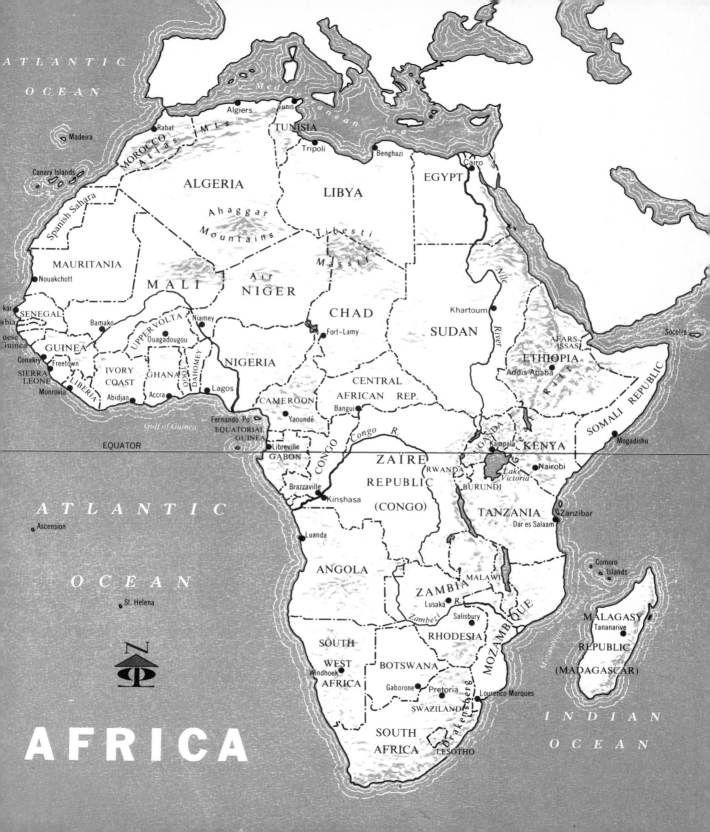

ATLANTIC

OCEAN

Madeira

Canary Islands

Spanish Sahara

MAURITANIA

Nouakchott

kar

SENEGAL

abia

uese

Guinea

Conakry

GUINEA

Freetown

SIERRA
LEONE

Monrovia

LIBERIA

Mediterranean Sea

Algiers

Tunis

TUNISIA

Tripoli

Benghazi

Cairo

Rabat

MOROCCO

Atlas Mts.

ALGERIA

LIBYA

EGYPT

*Ahaggar
Mountains*

*Tibesti
Massif*

Air

MALI

NIGER

CHAD

SUDAN

Khartoum

Nile

River

AFARS-
ISSAS

Socotra

ETHIOPIA

Addis Ababa

SOMALI REPUBLIC

Bamako

Niamey

UPPER VOLTA

Ouagadougou

TOGO

DAHOMEY

NIGERIA

Fort-Lamy

CENTRAL
AFRICAN REP.

IVORY
COAST

GHANA

Accra

Abidjan

Lagos

CAMEROON

Bangui

Yaoundé

Gulf of Guinea

Fernando Po

EQUATORIAL
GUINEA

EQUATOR

Libreville

GABON

Congo R.

Congo

ZAIRE

REPUBLIC

(CONGO)

UGANDA

Kampala

*Lake
Victoria*

KENYA

Nairobi

Mogadishu

RWANDA

BURUNDI

TANZANIA

Zanzibar

Dar es Salaam

Brazzaville

Kinshasa

ATLANTIC

OCEAN

Ascension

St. Helena

Luanda

ANGOLA

ZAMBIA

MALAWI

Lusaka

Zambezi R.

Salisbury

RHODESIA

MOZAMBIQUE

Comoro
Islands

MALAGASY

Tananarive

REPUBLIC

(MADAGASCAR)

SOUTH
WEST
AFRICA

Windhoek

BOTSWANA

Gaborone

Pretoria

Lourenco Marques

Drakersberg

SWAZILAND

SOUTH
AFRICA

LESOTHO

AFRICA

INDIAN

OCEAN

N
S

Enchantment of Africa

MOROCCO

by ALLAN CARPENTER
and JANIS FORTMAN

Consulting Editor
Donna Maier-Weaver
Fellow, Department of History
Northwestern University
Evanston, Illinois

 CHILDRENS PRESS, CHICAGO

THE ENCHANTMENT OF AFRICA

Available now: Botswana, Burundi, Egypt, Kenya, Lesotho, Liberia, Mali, Malagasy Republic (Madagascar), Morocco, Rhodesia, Rwanda, Sierra Leone, Swaziland, Tanzania, Tunisia, Uganda, Upper Volta, Zaïre Republic (Congo Kinshasa), Zambia
Planned for the future: Algeria, Cameroon, Central African Republic, Chad, Congo (Brazzaville), Dahomey, Equatorial Guinea, Ethiopia, Gambia, Gabon, Ghana, Guinea, Ivory Coast, Libya, Malawi, Mauritania, Niger, Nigeria, Senegal, Somali Republic, South Africa, Sudan, Togo

ACKNOWLEDGMENTS

M. Mekki Zailachi, Embassy of Morocco, Washington, D.C.; Albert W. Dalgliesh, Jr., Embassy of the U.S.A., Rabat, Morocco; Boufiaue Mohamed, Office National Marocain du Tourisme, Rabat, Morocco.

Cover Photograph: Street scene in Fez, Allan Carpenter
Frontispiece: Oasis of Tiznit, Office National Marocain du Tourisme

Project Editor: Joan Downing
Assistant Editor: Diane Salyers
Manuscript Editor: Elizabeth Rhein
Map Artist: Donald G. Bouma

LIBRARY OF CONGRESS
CATALOGING IN PUBLICATION DATA

Carpenter, John Allan, 1917-
    Morocco
    (Enchantment of Africa)
    SUMMARY: An introduction to the geography, history, government, economy, culture, people, and major cities of the westernmost Arab nation in North Africa.
    1. Morocco—Juvenile literature. [1. Morocco] I. Fortman, Janis, joint author II. Title.
DT305. C26   964   7511694
ISBN 0-516-04577-6

Contents

A True Story to Set the Scene

"RAISULI DEAD OR PERDICARIS ALIVE!"

In 1904 an American named Ion Perdicaris and his British son-in-law were kidnapped in Tangier, Morocco, by a bandit named Raisuli. It wasn't long before the whole world knew about the kidnapping. In the United States, corner newsboys shouted the headlines: "Raisuli dead or Perdicaris alive!" British and American warships were sent to the bay at Tangier. The people of Tangier panicked, deserted their houses, and fled from the city. For this kidnapping was no ordinary kidnapping, and Raisuli was no ordinary bandit.

As the head of the Idrisite dynasty, Raisuli had been born into a high social position. But he was also a *sherif* (a descendant of Muhammad, the Prophet of Islam, founder of the Islam religion). In a country where everyone follows Islam, this fact made Raisuli a very influential man. Also, Raisuli was a theologian (student of religions), having studied in Cairo, the capital of Egypt. Some people even called him *cid,* or "saint." Raisuli was respected and admired by many Moroccans.

In spite of his social position and education, Raisuli became a cattle thief and bandit. He stole from the rich Moroccans and Europeans and gave to poor local

Many towns in Morocco are enclosed in high walls. The town where Raisuli was imprisoned had a city gate much like this one.

MICHAEL ROBERTS

7

people. In time, Raisuli was caught by the Moroccan government and imprisoned in the worst prison in all of Morocco. In his dark, damp dungeon, Raisuli was fed only meager amounts of bread and water. But eventually one of his friends managed to slip a file into a piece of bread. For the next five months, Raisuli worked slavishly at night, filing at his chains and fetters. Finally he cast them off and broke out of prison. Unfamiliar with the city's narrow, winding streets, Raisuli became confused. Then he heard the prison alarm sound and the city gates close. In his panic, Raisuli ran into an alley with no outlet, where he was captured and dragged back to prison.

Locked in even stronger chains, Raisuli spent the next two years in the dungeon, ill with fever. Only through the persistent efforts of a powerful friend was he finally released.

Once again free, Raisuli found that the government had confiscated all of his wealth and property. Enraged, he returned to his life as a bandit, determined to somehow regain what was his. After a while, Raisuli began a life of kidnapping. His first well-known hostage, in 1903, was the Tangier correspondent for the London *Times*, Walter B. Harris. Raisuli demanded a high ransom for this hostage, and got it. The Moroccan government sent troops after Raisuli, but the local people liked Raisuli and warned him of the troops' attacks, and he was able to escape.

Raisuli's great influence over the local tribesmen was aided by his appearance. He was a well-built man with a dark beard and mustache. A long braid on an otherwise shaven head was tucked under a dark blue turban. Raisuli's short brown *djellaba* (hooded cloak) reached his knees, leaving his legs bare, and on his feet he wore a pair of yellow *babouches* (slippers). Dressed in this fashion, Raisuli looked more like a religious man than a monk does.

One night in May of 1904, Raisuli and his band of barbarous-looking men broke into the drawing room of a luxurious country mansion outside Tangier. The men bound Ion Perdicaris and his son-in-law and marched them over wild hills. Though he was a captive, Perdicaris was treated quite well. He was invited to Raisuli's feasts and spent many absorbing hours listening to the bandit's fantastic stories of the olden days of Arabia. According to Perdicaris and Raisuli's later hostages, the bandits were all very pleasant.

Raisuli made outrageous ransom demands: dismiss the governor of Tangier; disband the Northern Moroccan army; release certain imprisoned tribesmen; imprison certain members of the government; appoint Raisuli governor of five northern districts in Morocco; and pay him a sum of $70,000.

The Moroccan, American, and British governments were enraged. For five weeks, they sent frantic messages back and forth. They knew that the Moroccan government itself was in a state of turmoil. It was too weak to capture Raisuli and too weak to protect the lives and property of

Europeans living in Tangier. So, unable to do anything else, the Moroccan government granted Raisuli's terms. He became governor of the area around Tangier. Now a wealthy leader, his prestige among the tribes became even greater.

Raisuli transformed a miserable Arab village called Zinat into his capital. He built a medieval-type castle there, complete with battlements and drawbridges. There was a great hall for prayers, dungeons filled with prisoners, and cellars stuffed with treasure. Local leaders flocked to Zinat, bringing tribute to the "king of the mountains of Morocco," as Raisuli called himself.

Raisuli was a strong and fair ruler. His bands policed the districts, making the roads safe for travel. In fact, not a single shipment was looted within his districts. Raisuli regulated the sanitation of the villages in his districts so well that the dreaded smallpox ceased to occur there. He taught women how to keep their babies' eyes clean, reducing the number of eye diseases.

But after a while Raisuli began to overdo things. He extended his authority to neighboring Tangier, cutting off its electric lights, flogging its "protected" natives, and blackmailing its Europeans. The foreign governments could not ignore these moves. Sending battleships into the bay at Tangier, they demanded that the Moroccan government end this state of affairs. The Moroccan government reacted immediately, sending troops to Zinat and destroying Raisuli's glorious castle with cannon and gunfire. Raisuli fled to the mountains, but he took along as a hostage Sir Harry MacLean, one of the sultan's British advisers. After seven months, MacLean was ransomed for $100,000.

Walter Harris, Ion Perdicaris, and Harry MacLean all had good relations with Raisuli. These Europeans, made hostages by Raisuli, later praised the bandit highly for his good breeding. Though they had been his kidnapping victims, these distinguished men came to regard Raisuli as a "perfect gentleman of his native land."

The Face of the Land

Jazirat-al-Maghreb, or "The Island of the West," is what the Arabs once called Morocco. Located on the northwest corner of Africa, Morocco is somewhat like an island. It is cut off by water on one side and desert on the other—the vast Sahara. Morocco's only neighbors are Algeria on the east and Spanish Sahara on the south. To the west is the Atlantic Ocean and to the north is the Mediterranean Sea.

The countryside near the coastal city of Rabat is thick with olive groves, apple and pear orchards, and vineyards.

Morocco is the closest African country to Europe: the distance across the Strait of Gibraltar from the southern tip of Spain to the northern tip of Morocco is only ten miles. Slightly larger than the states of Washington and Oregon combined, Morocco's area is 172,414 square miles.

LAND

Morocco is divided into five geographic regions: the Rif mountains, the western plains and plateaus, the Atlas Mountains, the pre-Sahara, and the eastern plateaus. The far-northern Rif mountains stretch along the Mediterranean coast for more than two hundred miles eastward from the Strait of Gibraltar. The Rif's highest peaks rise to seven thousand feet. Within the range are deep, rugged valleys, dug away by hundreds of generations of erosion. The slopes of the Rif are covered with pine forests.

Along the Atlantic coast from Tangier to Essaouira stretch flat, lush plains. This coastal plain is heavily populated. The land is thick with olive groves, apple and pear orchards, and vineyards. To the east of the plains is the coastal plateau, or *meseta,* which varies in height from eighteen hundred to three thousand feet.

11

East of the meseta, the land rises and quickly becomes mountainous. The Atlas Mountains are about 125 miles inland, dividing the country between the Mediterranean world of the north and the desert world of the south. The Atlas Mountains are broken up into three areas: High Atlas, Middle Atlas, and Anti-(Lower) Atlas. The Middle Atlas extends south of the Rif, and includes all of central Morocco. The average altitude of the Middle Atlas is four thousand feet, though a few peaks rise to ten thousand feet. In this region, green pastures and clear lakes are surrounded by oak, pine, and cedar forests.

The Taza corridor divides the Middle Atlas from the High Atlas, a higher and more rugged part of the Atlas range. The highest peaks in North Africa are found in the High Atlas: Djebel Toubkal (13,600 feet) and Irhil M'Goun (13,300 feet). The High Atlas reaches the ocean just south of Essaouira, dividing the northern coastal plains from the Anti-Atlas to the south.

There are no high peaks in the Anti-Atlas. This part of the mountain range looks like a high, barren platform. South and east of the Anti-Atlas, the land drops to the *hammadas*, the rocky desert areas of the pre-Sahara. The Draâ River cuts through this area, flowing east to the desert plateau. Along the river people live in *ksours* (fortified villages), which overlook the river and the lush gardens of date palms and roses.

RIVERS

Morocco has the most extensive river system in all of North Africa. The rivers all rise in the Atlas and the Rif, ending either in the Mediterranean Sea, the Atlantic Ocean, or the Sahara.

MAP KEY

Agadir, E2
Agdz, E4
Ahfir, B6
Al Hoceima, B5
Alnif, D4
Anti-Atlas, E3
Asilah, B4
Atlas Mountains, D4
Azemmour, C3
Azrou, C4
Bay of Agadir, E2
Béchar, D6
Beni-Guil, D5
Běni-Mellal, D4
Ben-Slimane, C4
Berguent, C6
Berkane, B6
Berrechid, C3
Bou Arfa, D6
Boudenib, D5
Bou Izakarn, E2
Boujad, C4
Bou Regrez River, C4
Cap des

Trois Fourches, B5
Cap Juby, F1
Cap Rhir, E2
Casablanca, C3
Ceuta (Sp.), B4
Chechaouene, B4
Daoura River, E5
Djebel Ayachi, D5
Djebel Toubkal, D3
Draâ River, E4
Draâ Valley, F3
El-Hajeb, C4
El-Jadida, C3
El-Kelaa-
  des-Srarhna, D3
El-Khemis, F1
Erfoud, D5
Essaouira, D2
Fez, C5
Figuig, D6
Fkih-Ben-Salah, D4
Foum-Zguid, E4
Gibraltar (U.K.), B4
Goulimine, E2

Guercif, C5
Guir River, D5
High Atlas, D4
Ifni, E2
Ifrane, C5
Imilchil, D3
Irhil M'Goun, D4
Itzer, C5
Jerada, C6
Kasba-Tadla, D4
Kenadsa, D6
Kenitra, C4
Khemisset, C4
Khenifra, C4
Khouribga, C4
Ksar-el-Kebir, B4
Ksar-es-Souk, D5
Larache, B4
Marrakech, D3
Martil River, B4
Matarka, C6
Meknès, C4
Melilla (Sp.), B5
Middle Atlas, C5

Midelt, D5
Mohammedia, C3
Moulay-Idriss, C4
Moulouya River, C5
Nador, B5
Ouarzazete, D4
Oued-Zem, C4
Ouezzane, B4
Oujda, C6
Ouled al-Hadj, C5
Oum er Rbia
  River, C3
Rabat, C4
Rharb, C4
Rif, B5
Rommani, C4
Safi, D3
Sahara Desert, E4, E5
Salé, C4
Sebjet Tah, F1
Sebou River, C4
Sefrou, C5
Settat, C3
Sidi-Kacem, C4

Sidi-Slimane, C4
Souk-el-Arba-
  du-Rharb, C4
Souss River, E3
Strait of
  Gibraltar, B4
Tafraoute, E3
Taguounite, E4
Tangier, B4
Tangier Bay, B4
Tan-Tan, F1
Taouz, D5
Tarfaya, F1
Taroudannt, E3
Tata, E3
Taza, C5
Tendrara, C6
Tensift River, D3
Tétouan, B4
Tinerhir, D4
Tiznit, E2
Youssoufia, D3
Zellija-Boubeker, C6
Ziz River, D5

PORTUGAL

S P A I N

O C E A N

MEDITERRANEAN SEA

GIBRALTAR (U.K.)
Strait of Gibraltar
Ceuta (Spain)
Alboran
(Spain)

Tangier Bay
Tangier
Tétouan
Martil River
Al Hoceima
Cap des Trois Fourches
Melilla (Spain)

Asilah
Chechaouene
Nador
Berkane
Ahfir

Larache
R I F
Oujda
Jerada
Zellija-Boubeker

Ksar-el-Kebir
Ouezzane
Guercif
RHARB
Souk-el-Arba-du-Rharb
Taza
Berguent

Kenitra
Sebou
River
Moulay-Idriss
Matarka

Sidi-Slimane
Sidi-
Kacem
Fez
MIDDLE ATLAS
M O U L O U Y A   River

RABAT
Salé
Khemisset
Meknès
Sefrou
Ouled al-Hadj

Mohammedia
Casablanca
El-Hajeb
Ifrane
Azrou

Ben-
Slimane
Rommani
Bou Regrez River
M O U N T A I N S
Tendrara

Azemmour
Berrechid
Itzer
Midelt
Beni-Guil
Bou Arfa

El-
Jadida
Settat
Oued-Zem
Khenifra
Djebel
Ayachi
Figuig

Safi
Khouribga
Boujad
Kasba-Tadla
Fkih-Ben-Salah
Ksar-es-Souk
Boudenib

Youssoufia
Beni-Mellal
Guir River
Béchar

El-Kelaa-des-Srarhna
H I G H   A T L A S   M O U N T A I N S
Kenadsa

Essaouira
Tensift River
Marrakech
Irhil M'Goun
Ziz River
Ksar-es-Souk

Imilchil
Tinerhir
Erfoud

Cap Rhir
Djebel Toubkal
Ouarzazete
Alnif
Taouz

Agadir
Taroudannt
Souss River
Agdz
Draâ
River
Daoura River
UNDEFINED
BOUNDARY

Bay of Agadir
ANTI-ATLAS
Foum-Zguid
D E S E R T

Tiznit
Tafraoute
Tata
Taguounite

Ifni

Bou Izakarn

Goulimine

CANARY
ISLANDS
Draâ
River
S A H A R A
V A L L E Y

Tan-Tan
DRAA

Cap Juby
Tarfaya
El-Khemis

Sebjet Tah

S P A N I S H

S A H A R A

MOROCCO

M A U R I T A N I A

A L G E R I A

Except for the Moulouya River, all the Mediterranean rivers rise in the Rif. None of these are important rivers, and the largest is only fifty miles long. They flow irregularly, and their beds cut deep gorges. Most of the time they are just dry, muddy, little creeks. But when it rains, they become raging torrents.

The Saharan rivers originate in the Atlas, thin out due to the intense desert heat, and disappear completely in the dry season. Even during the wet season, they flow only sporadically. Water is also lost through the intensive irrigation in the pre-Saharan oases.

Like the other rivers in Morocco, those that flow to the Atlantic are usually very dry and sluggish. During the rainy season, however, their sources become violent, fast-moving rivers that create great danger of floods. By the time these rivers reach the plains, however, they have lost much of their force and volume. Many converge before reaching the ocean.

CLIMATE

There are four distinctive weather regions in Morocco: coastal, interior, mountain, and Saharan. The Atlantic coastal

Throughout southern Morocco, people live in fortified villages called ksours.

OFFICE NATIONAL MAROCAIN DU TOURISME

The Atlantic coastal region of Morocco has a warm, sunny climate year-round.

region has a mild, sunny climate, with about three hundred days of sun each year and warm temperatures year-round. In the interior region, however, temperature varies greatly—not just between summer and winter, but also between night and day. The mountain region has much snow and rain in winter and many storms in summer. The Saharan region is very dry all year, with almost no rain.

Throughout the country, summers are hot and dry, except along the humid Mediterranean coast. This is partly due to a Saharan wind called the *sirocco* which sweeps through the country periodically during the summer. The only place not strongly affected by the sirocco is the higher mountain area. Summer days there

are cool and nights are cold. The mountains also receive Morocco's only summer rain.

Fall brings occasional rain to the country. The temperature averages about sixty-eight degrees Fahrenheit, but in the mountains the temperature sometimes drops to zero. In the winter, westerly winds off the Atlantic bring rain to the interior and snow to the mountains. But the mountains stop these winds from traveling farther, and the pre-Sahara remains dry. The mountain snows melt in the spring, causing serious floods in the interior region, especially in the Rharb Plain. But snow remains all year on the peak of Djebel Ayachi, at the eastern end of the High Atlas.

15

Four Children of Morocco

SAID OF IMILCHIL

High in the Atlas Mountains, nestled amid open pastures and thick cedar forests, lies the little village of Imilchil. Here red-earth buildings cluster inside a fortresslike wall of the same red earth— built as a fortification against attackers. Towering above the village are treeless, snow-capped peaks. The sky glows orange with evening, for the sun fell behind the mountain peaks many hours earlier.

It is March, and the snow on the mountains is already melting. The little streams have become wild with the torrents of icy water. In a stream near the village, a boy named Said (pronounced *sayeed*) dives

Said lives in the village of Imilchil, high in the Atlas Mountains.

OFFICE NATIONAL MAROCAIN DU TOURISME

into the water. He quickly splashes to the bank; shivering, he climbs out and puts on his clothes. Gathering his flock of sheep, which have been grazing all afternoon in a pasture, he leads them to the village.

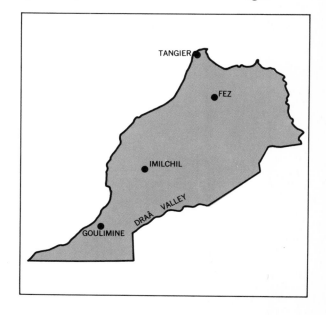

Nearing his house, Said smells dinner cooking. His mother has spent the whole day preparing the meal. There is roast mutton, white cheese, *couscous* (steamed hominy), bread made of barley meal, and goat's milk. After dinner is eaten, there will be a ritual of mint tea, the national drink of Morocco.

Said, like most Moroccans, is a Muslim. The only school he attends is a religious class held on Friday afternoons. The religious leader of the village teaches Said and other boys the tenets of the Islam religion and the words of the prophet Muhammad as well as the history of Morocco and the Berber peoples.

Before the first sign of daybreak, Said and his family are already working. It is Thursday—market day in this remote part of Morocco. Since the *souk,* or marketplace, is fourteen miles away, Said and his family must get an early start. Said's mother prepares breakfast while Said and his father pack the donkeys and horses. Atop the colorful saddles and blankets, Said places bags filled with wool and dried skins. Said's baby sister is carried in a *snood* on his mother's back.

It is Said's responsibility to lead the family to the souk, and he follows a path he knows quite well. They pass over a steep, rocky trail and soon meet other families who are also on their way to the souk. A small caravan forms—people, donkeys, horses, and mules, all laden with goods. Finally the caravan arrives at the marketplace. The rest of the week, this dusty clearing is inhabited only by crows and wild pigeons, but on Thursdays it is crowded with people, animals, and goods to be sold.

The sky is already light with early morning. Said's family got there very early this morning and were able to find a corner spot, the best selling place in the market. First Said helps his father set up the tent and then he places the dried skins on a carpet spread over the ground. Said puts his baby sister on a straw mat on the ground, where she will sleep most of the day. Free to spend the rest of the day as he likes, Said sets off to look for his friends.

Khalifa and Driss are already waiting for Said. Sauntering down the souk's narrow aisles, the boys talk excitedly about what they've been doing. They pass farmers selling barley, vegetables, and fruit; shepherds selling wool, sheep, and goats; and weavers selling cloth. All the merchants wear brown *djellabas* (long, loose garments with full sleeves and hoods) and ankle-length robes. Over their shaved heads they wear turbans. The women all wear brightly colored orange, blue, and scarlet beads over their *caftans* (cotton or silk ankle-length garments with full sleeves).

Said, Khalifa, and Driss stop at the barber's stall, where they have their heads shaved. As usual, the barber leaves a single lock of hair on the boys' heads. Said knows the legend behind this lock, called the Handle of the Prophet. If a boy is sick or has an accident, Muhammad will grab the boy by that lock and pull him to heaven.

On market day, people from remote villages in the Atlas Mountains travel to the souk *(marketplace) to sell their goods.*

By noon the souk is crowded with people bustling, chattering, and bargaining furiously. The boys stop at the shop of the medicine man. As always, they are intrigued by what they find there. Spread on the carpet are dried toads, spiders, grasshoppers, and the head of a hyena. Hanging from the ropes are dead birds, dried snakes, and lizards. Said is most fascinated with the snakeskin of the Taroudannt cobra, used to cure a headache or a sore throat. If the person has a headache, the skin is worn around the person's head; if the person has a sore throat, the skin is worn around his neck.

The sound of music distracts Said from the medicines. As he turns around, he sees four flutists and a few dancers. The boys watch for a while, then start back. When Said reaches his father's stand, it is already late. Hurriedly, he helps take down the tent and pack the animals with the goods that were not sold. The sun is setting as the family starts the journey home.

19

DAIWA OF FEZ

In the old section of Fez, white buildings reflect the hot, midafternoon sun. Narrow alleys are wedged between high concrete walls. Only the heavy wooden doors with iron knockers hint at the great luxury inside the walls, where courtyards filled with blooming jasmines, poppies, and roses surround gurgling fountains. Luxurious two-story houses overlook the lush courtyards.

In one of these elegant old houses, a girl named Daiwa leans dreamily out of an upstairs window. On the chair beside her lays a piece of half-embroidered cloth. Slowly, Daiwa turns back to the room, taking off her yellow silk caftan and replacing it with her street dress, a white djellaba that reaches her ankles. She places a veil over her face.

Daiwa spends most of her time inside the house, helping the maids with small tasks or working on her embroidery. Over the years, Daiwa has spent many hours embroidering cushions, linen, and cloth. These now lie in a large chest, waiting for Daiwa's wedding day, when they will be put in her new house. Daiwa's wedding was arranged by her parents when she was quite young. In two years, when Daiwa is fourteen, she will be married. Daiwa has not seen the man she will marry since they were both small children. Nor has Daiwa ever been to school.

When she finishes dressing, Daiwa leaves the house and heads for the souk. She strolls along the street, passing cafes and shops, speaking to no one. Her thoughts are of tomorrow's *diffa* (meal). Daiwa's father, a prominent businessman who deals in fine silks, has invited a few of his customers and friends over for the meal. Daiwa will spend the whole day helping her mother and the maids prepare the diffa, but as Muslim tradition dictates, Daiwa and her mother will not be allowed to eat with the guests. Lamb roasted with prunes, onions, and olives will be served with bowls of yogurt. The second course will include *tajine* (chickens roasted in oil with apples), as well as carrots, green olives, and crusty, fresh-baked bread.

For the last course, mutton couscous will be served. The guests will eat it with their fingers, rolling the couscous into tiny balls and popping it into their mouths. For dessert, there will be black coffee and pastries filled with almonds and honey. As always, the ritual of mint tea will conclude the diffa.

Suddenly, Daiwa is brought back to the present by the smell of fresh mint, which fills the air. The souk of Fez covers many blocks and each block sells only one kind of product. As Daiwa enters the souk, she

In the old section of Fez, where Daiwa lives, narrow alleys are wedged between high concrete walls.

MICHAEL ROBERTS

20

At one end of the souk is the copper lane, where copper wares
hang from the stalls, reflecting the bright sunlight.

is surrounded by brightly colored prayer rugs hanging from the shops. People and animals all squeeze through the souk's narrow lanes. At the end of the block is the copper lane, where copper wares hang from the stalls, reflecting the bright sunlight. Daiwa turns into another lane, this one filled with piles of woven baskets. Finally, Daiwa reaches the spice bazaar. Here rows of bins overflow with colorful spices: sage, thyme, saffron, coriander, cloves, and paprika.

Daiwa asks a merchant for saffron and paprika; then she and the merchant haggle over a price. After some bargaining, the price is set. Daiwa smiles because she knew all along what the price would be. But bargaining is an expected practice, and it makes shopping more pleasant. As the merchant weighs the spices and wraps them in brown paper, his donkey stands quietly next to the stand.

Daiwa knows that she is expected home quickly, but she does not want to leave the market without listening to the storyteller. Quickly, she passes the lane of vegetable stands and baskets of sticky dates, entering the public square. She spots a group of people sitting on the ground around the storyteller. Daiwa joins the group just as the old man begins the story of the wasp.

"Allah created the world," the storyteller begins. "He created the skies, the stars, the earth, and the waters. He brought in light and dark to divide the day. Then Allah added grass, fruits, flowering plants, and trees. The world was beautiful but it needed movement. So Allah added living creatures: horses, donkeys, sheep, birds, dogs, fish, ants— and many other animals.

"Then Allah asked each animal what it wanted to do in the world and promised that each animal would get its wish. The little wasp thought and thought. Finally he decided. He wished that any animal he stung would die immediately.

"The wasp listened to all the other animals state their wishes, and he saw Allah grant all the wishes. Finally it was his turn. The wasp meant to say: 'He who I sting shall die.' But he was flustered and made a mistake. Instead, he said: 'After I sting I shall die.' The wasp tried to correct himself, but it was too late. As Allah had promised, the wish had already been granted.

"That is why wasps die after they sting someone," the storyteller concludes and everyone begins to clap, clamoring for more stories. The story was a long one, though, and Daiwa is already late. She knows her mother is waiting for the spices so she can start preparing tomorrow's diffa. Smiling, Daiwa turns around and heads for home.

AHMED OF THE DRAÂ VALLEY

As the caravan slowly snakes its way across the blistering desert, the hot sun dries up the last few drops of water. The temperature is 120 degrees. A strong gust of wind throws particles of sand into the air, shifting the dunes into new shapes.

In the caravan, a boy named Ahmed wipes the sand from his eyes, realizing how tired and thirsty he is. There had been no water at the last watering spot, which meant that it had been four days since the camels had had any water. Ahmed knows that these camels can last only five days without water. He looks at his camel: the hump on the short-furred, slender animal has almost disappeared and Ahmed wonders how long his animal will last. There just has to be water at the next watering spot.

After a few hours, the caravan reaches the watering place. The sun is already sinking into the night. Ahmed hears one of the men yell that the well has water. Allah be praised, Ahmed thinks. The animals are saved!

Ahmed loosens his camel and lets it drink some water. Then he cleans himself in the sand and, as always, bends down, head touching the ground, toward Mecca to pray until the sun disappears into the night. Then Ahmed and his family eat a meal of mashed barley and lie on the ground to sleep.

The next morning they arise at dawn. The camel market will begin the next day, so they must reach Goulimine by dusk. An

Left: A Berber girl from the "Blue Men" tribe of Goulimine. Opposite: In Goulimine, the camel market is an annual affair.

annual affair, the camel market is held early in the year, after the corn harvest. Berbers come from the Atlas and nomads come from the desert to sell their camels. This annual gathering was originally a pilgrimage: Muslims came to the grave of a *marabout* (a holy man) to pray. But over the years, the pilgrimage gradually became a time of trade and amusement.

Although the sun has hardly risen over the land, the day is already scorching hot, just like any other. Ahmed finds his place in the caravan as it begins the day's journey. In front and in back of him, next to the camels and goats, men, women, and children walk, their blue robes flowing in the wind. Because their skins are tinted blue, this tribe is called the "Blue Men."

Ahmed knows the story behind his people's blue-tinted skins. In the fifteenth century, an Englishman introduced blue cotton cloth to the people who lived at the port of Agadir. Ahmed's ancestors liked the cloth because its indigo dye rubbed off on their skin. Ever since, the "Blue Men" have continued to buy this particular cloth, and over the many years, their skin has gradually become pigmented by the dye. Ahmed has learned that the more dye that rubs off a piece of fabric, the more valuable the cloth is considered to be.

Late in the afternoon, the caravan reaches the oasis village of Goulimine, stopping on the outskirts of the village. Ahmed helps his father set up their goat-hair tent, since they will be staying here

24

for a week. Ahmed lays the beautiful carpets on the floor inside and puts the family's possessions in their proper places. In the center of the tent, his mother fills a bowl with dates, almonds, and a block of sugar. Ahmed scatters the family's many embroidered ram skins about the tent. The family's clothes and supplies are stored in these skins. In the back of the tent, Ahmed places the embroidered cushions.

Outside, Ahmed's mother begins to cook dinner. Into the *guedra* (the family cooking pot) she places goat meat, onions, and chick-peas and begins to steam them in water.

The next morning, Ahmed awakes to the sound of braying camels. The streets of Goulimine are jammed with the animals, running loose but guarded by their owners. On the sides of the streets are traders from stockyards in the north. They watch the parade of camels, studying each animal carefully. When a trader wants to buy a camel, he and the owner haggle over a price. Then comes Ahmed's favorite part of the trade: the buyer hires a *gabbadh* (camel cowboy) to catch the spirited camel.

Across the road, Ahmed notices some gabbadhs working. He hurries over and is just in time to see a gabbadh place his lasso on the dusty ground. The camel is driven toward the loop of the lasso by another boy. When the camel walks into the loop, the gabbadh pulls the rope sharply, snaring the animal's hind leg. At the same time, the other boy leaps on the camel's neck, almost strangling it. Groaning, the camel falls to the ground. Quickly, the gabbadh ties up one of the animal's front legs. Ahmed watches as the new owner leads the camel peacefully away, and is amazed at the skill and speed of the gabbadh, who is only a few years older than Ahmed.

Slowly Ahmed walks back to his tent. Camel market is perhaps his favorite time of the year, but he is anxious to be back home. With the money that his father gets from the camels, his mother will buy dates, barley, sugar, and tea. At the end of the week, Ahmed and his people will pack their animals and leave Goulimine, setting off once again across the desert to their meager pastures in the Draâ Valley.

RHIMA OF TANGIER

Along the clear, blue waters of the Strait of Gibraltar lies the famed city of Tangier. Boats docked in the harbor move rhythmically with the waves against a backdrop of ultramodern buildings. White skyscrapers pierce the cloudless blue sky.

It is only May, but already the weather is hot. The sun is high in the sky. Midafternoon noises are interrupted as school bells sound throughout the city. Then the school doors swing open as children pour out onto the streets. One of the stragglers is a miniskirted Arab girl named Rhima. Under her arm she carries a French record, which a girlfriend has loaned her for the weekend.

On the way home, Rhima weaves through the crowds on the busy street. She notices the difference in dress among the people: there are veiled Arab women, men in white djellabas, women in short skirts, and men in business suits. Rhima passes office buildings, a movie theater, a few boutiques, and French cafes crammed with people reading papers, sipping drinks, or talking excitedly. Waiting on the corner for the green light, Rhima sees that the traffic is jammed once again. All kinds of automobiles—Italian Fiats, French Renaults, German Opels, and British Austins —wedge around each other, horns blaring. Rhima laughs as she crosses the street, knowing that she will reach the end of the block before any of the cars do.

Rhima enters a tall apartment building and steps into the elevator. She had almost forgotten about the record under her arm, but now she can't wait to hear it! Rushing into her room, she turns on the record player, but soon she's interrupted by her mother calling. The soccer game! In her excitement about the record, Rhima had completely forgotten—tonight the Tangier team is playing Rabat.

Both of Rhima's parents are already home from the hospital, where Rhima's father works as a doctor and her mother as a research assistant. Her parents met many years before when they were studying medicine at a university in France. Rhima is proud that both her parents have such important jobs. Rhima, too, hopes to go to a French university, but she does not yet know what she wants to study—perhaps

As Rhima walks down the street, she notices the difference in dress among the people.

medicine or education, or maybe even law.

Dinner is already on the table as Rhima sits down next to her younger brother. The cook has prepared onion soup, a tomato salad, lamb chops, and string beans. For dessert, there are pastries and fruit. After dinner, the family leaves for the game.

The stadium is packed when Rhima's family arrives and the team is already walking onto the field. Hurrying, they find their seats just as the game is beginning. The kickoff is a long one, and a Rabat man catches the ball on the twenty-five-yard line. He runs fifteen yards, is tackled, and the men all fall in a heap. The game has begun!

Rhima's father, an avid soccer fan, has been trying to teach Rhima the rules of the game. But Rhima still does not understand everything that happens. Sometimes she loses track of who has the ball and follows someone else, only to discover that the person who did have the ball has already been tackled! But it does not matter to Rhima that she cannot always follow the

Soccer is one of Morocco's most popular sports.

ROYAUME DU MAROC MINISTERE DE L'INFORMATION

Rhima will spend the next day at one of Morocco's many beautiful beaches.

game, for she enjoys watching the spectators most of all. Sometimes they get so angry! People jump up and down, screaming and shouting, as if they are actually playing. All this excitement is contagious, though, and soon Rhima, too, is jumping and screaming.

Before Rhima knows it, the game is almost over. With only one minute left in the game, the score is Tangier-14, Rabat-17. Tangier has the ball on its twenty-yard line. Rhima knows that there is still a chance to win the game if only the Tangier team can get a touchdown. As the seconds

tick away, the crowd tenses. Rhima holds her breath. With only fifteen seconds left, Tangier kicks the ball. Over the goal post it goes! A touchdown! The crowd goes wild—the Tangier team has won!

Rhima and her family follow the many people out of the stadium. It was an exciting game, but Rhima is tired and can hardly wait to get home. Tomorrow will be a quieter day. There is no school, so she will meet several of her friends at the beach and spend the day there, lying in the warm sun and swimming in the oceanside pool.

Morocco Yesterday

The earliest inhabitants of Morocco were the Berbers. No one knows where they originated, but it is known that they have roamed the plains, mountains, and deserts of North Africa for more than seven thousand years.

EARLY TRADERS

Traders from Phoenicia built ports on the Mediterranean coast as early as the twelfth century B.C. Two hundred years later, they founded Carthage (in present-day Tunisia).

By 400 B.C. the Carthaginians dominated the entire Moroccan coast and built cities there. They were traders, not conquerors, and they made trade agreements with the local Berber herdsmen and farmers and friendship treaties with the local Berber leaders. Neither Phoenician nor Carthaginian traders ever ventured into the interior of Morocco.

AFRICA NOVA

In 146 B.C., the Romans defeated Carthage, pushing the boundaries of the Roman Empire westward. Soon Carthage's trading cities in northern Morocco were under Roman control. In 45 B.C., Julius Caesar gave the name "Africa Nova" to his holdings in northwestern Africa. Juba II, the son of a Berber king who had

The Roman settlement of Chellah, near Rabat, was once a part of Africa Nova.

become an ally of Caesar, became Africa Nova's ruler in 30 B.C. and reigned peacefully for forty-eight years.

In 40 A.D. Africa Nova was divided into two provinces. The western province was called Mauretania Tingitana. It included the northwestern part of present-day Morocco, stretching from eastern Morocco's Moulouya River west to the Atlantic Ocean, and from the Mediterranean Sea south to the city of Rabat. The name *Morocco* is derived from the word *Mauretania,* which means "land of the Maures" (Moors).

Rome governed Mauretania Tingitana for two centuries. But there was repeated Berber resistance to the Romans in much of the territory, especially in the south. By the third century A.D., Rome had pulled back to the area around Tangier.

The independent Berber tribes continued to resist the invaders that followed the Romans: the Gothic Vandals, who came in 429; the Byzantines of the sixth century; and the Islamic Arabs of the seventh century. Though the Berbers were successful in combating the Vandals and the Byzantines, they finally were conquered by the Arabs.

MOROCCO BECOMES MUSLIM

The religion of Islam was founded in 622 by a man named Muhammad, who lived in Arabia. In just a few years, this new faith had expanded across North Africa. Though the Sahara had previously blocked most invaders, it was no barrier to the Arabs. Living in the deserts of the Middle East, the Arabs were used to the hot, parched land with its seemingly endless miles of sand. Though the deserts were no obstacle, Morocco's Berbers were. Just as they had fought other invaders, the Berbers fought the Arabs. Finally, in 638, the Arabs had their first successful expedition into what they called the *Maghreb,* or "west," crossing the Taza Gap into the plains.

In the early eighth century, Arab armies completed their conquest of the Maghreb. Many of the Berbers were converted to Islam. In 711 these converts were enlisted to help in the conquest of Spain, and it was only a few years until they had conquered the whole Iberian Peninsula. They called this new Muslim province Andalusia.

The next period in Morocco's history was one of violent religious revolts. While Morocco was being conquered, Islam had split into two sects—the Sunnites and the Shiites. It was the Shiites who had originally conquered Morocco, followed by the Omayyads, who were Sunnite Muslims. In 740 the Berbers revolted against Arab domination and joined with another sect, the Kharedjites. Although the Berber revolts were suppressed, the Omayyad caliphate never regained complete power in Morocco.

In the mid-700s there was another struggle for the caliphate in the Middle East. The struggle ended when the Abassids overthrew the Omayyads in 750, and claimed the caliphate. Only one descendant of the Omayyad dynasty survived. He fled west to Morocco, and with the support of the Berbers, invaded Andalusia. By 756 Andalusia had become an Omayyad empire.

About 785, in the Middle East, the Shiites revolted against the Abassids, who had conquered them only about thirty-five years earlier. The revolt was suppressed. Its leader, Idrisid ibn Abdullah (usually called Idris I), fled west to North Africa. Reaching Morocco, he soon gained the acceptance of the Berbers in the north, becoming their ruler, or *imam*. Idris I converted more people to the Islam faith than any other Arab ruler had done, and is considered the "father of Morocco."

Afraid of Idris's power, the Abassid caliph sent a man to kill him. This man disguised himself as a refugee and was accepted into the court of Idris I. In 792, after having inspired Idris's confidence, the man poisoned him.

Idris's successors brought many more Arabic ways to Morocco. His son, Idris II, built a great capital at Fez. His grandson, Muhammad, formed an Arab government. The Idrisid dynasty lasted until the tenth century, when it was threatened by the Fatimids (Berbers from Algeria) and the Omayyads.

THE ALMORAVIDES

During the tenth and eleventh centuries, there was much rivalry in Morocco between the three main Berber groups. The Masmouda had inhabited the northwestern plains of Morocco for centuries.

FROM **MOROCCO AFTER 25 YEARS**, 1912

A typical Berber.

Now the Zenata were moving into this northern plain, and the Sanhaja were moving into the southern oases and eastern Morocco near the Moulouya River. The Zenata and Sanhaja were traditional enemies. Also, Bedouin Arabs from the Middle East were invading North Africa. Many settled in northern Morocco, spreading the Arabic language.

In the eleventh century, many Sanhajas began to accept the teachings of three warrior monks, who had formed a *ribat* (religious retreat) on the coast of Senegal. The group began to be called the

33

Almoravides (a Spanish corruption of *al murabitun,* or "men of the ribat"; the singular of this word is Almoravid). The Almoravides spread out from the ribat and other outposts to conquer Sanhaja tribes throughout southern Morocco. By 1060, in the name of their orthodox form of Islam, the Almoravides were fighting a *jihad* (holy war) in the northern plains. Their leader was now Yusuf ibn-Tashfin, who founded Marrakech as his capital in 1062. Within twenty-four years, the Almoravides had unified all of present-day Morocco under their form of Islam. They had also conquered the land south to Senegal, east to Algiers, and north to Saragossa (Spain).

THE ALMOHADES

The Almoravides had become more and more corrupt since the original campaign of the warrior monks. By 1100 many Moroccans were becoming disillusioned with the Almoravid rulers and their form of Islam. In the early twelfth century, a new kind of Islam was introduced by a scholar named Muhammad ibn-Tubart. He came from the Middle East to settle at Tinmel in the Atlas Mountains, where he talked of revolt against the Almoravides. Soon he gained supporters among the Masmouda Berbers in the Atlas. Muhammad ibn-Tubart and his followers were called the Almohades (from *al muhadin,* or "those of unity").

First the Almohades conquered the mountains; then they attacked Fez and Meknès; in 1147 they attacked Marrakech, killing the last of the Almoravid rulers. The Almohades extended their empire to the cities of Castile (Spain) in the north and Tripoli (Libya) in the east. They were the first to establish a central government in Morocco (the *makhzen*) which kept public order, enforced laws, and collected taxes. But the Almohades soon ran into the same problems that the Almoravides had encountered: Christian armies were invading Andalusia and Arab Bedouins were invading northern Morocco.

THE MERINIDES

In the early thirteenth century, the empire of the Almohades slowly began to fall. First they were defeated in Spain by Catholic kings. Later, when attacked by Arabs in Morocco, the Almohades asked a Zenata Berber people, the Beni Merin, for help. The Beni Merin knew that the Almohades were declining in power, so they agreed to help while actually planning to take control of the empire. They moved west over the Atlas, conquering as they went. In 1269 they captured Marrakech, and later killed the Almohad sultan.

This third great Berber dynasty was called the Merinid, after the name Beni Merin. It was based on unity of the people rather than religious reform, as the other two Berber dynasties had been. The empire of the Merinides never extended as far as the Almohad empire had. By the fourteenth century, the Merinid empire reached to Algeria in the east and to Granada (in present-day Spain), then the most wealthy and important city in the Arab world.

Art and education flourished under the Merinides. The empire lasted a century and a half. In 1465, another Zenata tribe, the Beni Wattas, ousted the Merinides and took control of the government. They allowed the Spanish and Portuguese to set up trading posts in towns along the Moroccan coast. But other Berber tribes repeatedly attacked the Europeans, forcing them to flee their Moroccan settlements. At the end of the fifteenth century, Andalusia was conquered by Spanish Christian armies. Thousands of Moriscos (Muslim Andalusians), who were being persecuted by the Christians moving into Andalusia, fled to Morocco.

THE SAADIANS

By 1511 many Muslims had begun to believe in the teachings of *marabouts* (holy men), "saints," and mystics. In that year, marabouts from the Draâ Valley called on the Saadian sherif to lead a jihad against the Portuguese. Though this war was unsuccessful, the sherif—and later his descendants—finally captured the city of Fez in 1549. This marked the beginning of the Saadian dynasty.

It was an uneasy beginning. For nearly thirty years, there was rivalry for the throne. Finally in 1578, Moulay Ahmad al-Mansur became sultan after killing all his rivals. He was the first Moroccan ruler

to use local officials to help him control the makhzen. Local governors called *pashas* oversaw the sultan's interests throughout the empire. A military was formed by recruiting groups called *guich* tribes. As payment, these men were exempt from taxes. Great golden mosques and palaces were constructed in Marrakech.

At this time in history, shipping on the Atlantic Ocean was frequently plagued by attacks from pirates. In 1627, Morisco pirates formed an independent republic near the cities of Rabat and Salé; they called it The Republic of the Two Shores. It became a base for pirates who plied the Atlantic, but was unsuccessful, coming to an end in 1641.

THE ALAOUITES

Other descendants of the Prophet were not living in such Saadian splendor, and they were not content. One of them, Moulay Rashid, captured northern Morocco in the mid-1600s. This ended the Saadian dynasty, and Moulay Rashid became the first Alaouite ruler. By 1670 he controlled all of Morocco.

His successor, Moulay Ismail, was possibly the greatest ruler Morocco ever had. When he became sultan in 1672, England, Portugal, and Spain were invading the coast, and groups of Berbers were rebelling throughout the Atlas. To quell these forces, Ismail raised an army of forty thousand black slaves from the Sudan. When they were not fighting, these slaves

The great mosque of Taroudannt was built during the Saadian dynasty.

constructed many *casbahs* (fortresses) throughout the country.

The sultan called his troops the "Black Guard," and in turn he was called the "Black Sultan," for he was a bloodthirsty ruler. Moulay Ismail and the "Black Guard" drove all the English, Spanish, Portuguese, Arabs, and Turks out of the country and stopped the local uprisings. Though Moulay Ismail hated Christianity, he was the first Moroccan ruler to recognize the importance of talking with non-Muslim nations. Meknès became his capital in 1673, and Moulay Ismail received many ambassadors there.

The European who most impressed the sultan was France's King Louis XIV. Moulay Ismail built a city at Meknès to rival King Louis's Versailles. Twenty-five thousand Christian slaves and thirty thousand Moroccan slaves labored to construct the city. They also spent many years building his vast palace, called Ville Imperiale, at nearby Fez. The ornately decorated Bab el Mansour (*bab* means gate) led into the palace. Below ground was a prison for Christians; above ground were splendid gardens and mazes of long, narrow hallways flanked by high walls. There were immense granaries and enormous stables and barracks for twelve thousand men of Ismail's "Black Guard." His reservoir was dug by hand by his thousands of slaves.

Moulay Ismail died in 1727 and for thirty years afterward there was fighting for the throne. In 1757 Sidi Muhammad Ben Abdallah put down Berber revolts in the Atlas. Soon he was accepted by the Berbers as their leader. As ruler, Sidi Muhammad Ben Abdallah continued relations with European countries. In a 1767 treaty, he expanded relations with the French, who had become the European country most closely associated with Morocco.

Because Moroccan pirates had been attacking and seizing American ships, in 1786 Muhammad Ben Abdallah extended a treaty of friendship to the United States —the Treaty of Marrakech. Another treaty, the Treaty of Meknès (1836), gave the United States more economic advantages in Morocco. This is the longest unbroken treaty relationship in United States history—it is still in effect.

THE EUROPEANS INTERVENE

In the late nineteenth century, three European nations—Britain, France, and Spain—wanted to increase their influence in Morocco. Britain had held Gibraltar, at Morocco's northern tip, since 1704, and wanted to keep control of the Strait of Gibraltar, an important passageway to the Middle East. France, which had captured Algeria in 1830, wanted to protect her North African empire and her trade interests in the Mediterranean. Spain felt that it was destined to control Morocco; in fact, Spain was the only one of the three European countries that directly controlled any Moroccan territory in the nineteenth century.

In 1880 a conference was held at Madrid, Spain, which was attended by twelve European nations, plus the United States and Morocco. At this conference, it was agreed that Morocco should remain independent.

During this period, there was no rule of succession. When a sultan died, a struggle for power ensued. In 1873 Sultan Moulay Hassan took the throne. He tried to maintain the unity of the country and introduce reforms. But he was generally unsuccessful, and he died in 1894. His successor, Abd al Aziz, was also eager to modernize Morocco. But he was an ineffective ruler and unable to carry through with his plans.

TURN OF THE CENTURY

Over the years the makhzen had become an orderly governmental system. Its strength depended on the power of the army and the ruling sultan. Laws were made by the sultan through *dahirs*, or royal decrees. The sultan's prime minister was called the *grand vizier*; other ministers were called *viziers*. Pashas and caids, positions established in the sixteenth century by the Saadian sultan Moulay Ahmad al-Mansur, had long since become hereditary positions, held by powerful local families.

Some Berber tribes would not submit to the sultan's rule. The area of these tribes was called *bled as-siba*, or "land of dissidence." The area of the central government was called *bled al-makhzen*.

These terms were used as far back as the twelfth century, when the Almohades first formed a strong central government under a sultan.

By the twentieth century the government was in a state of turmoil and the sultan Abd al Aziz had become unpopular. There had been many disturbances along the Morocco-Algeria border, and it had become increasingly difficult for independent Morocco to exist peaceably next to French Algeria.

Treaties with other European countries in the early twentieth century gave France the impetus to move into Morocco. These treaties maintained that other countries, including Italy and Great Britain, would recognize France's interests in Morocco if France would recognize their interests in other areas of Africa.

Thus, France moved into some areas of northeast Morocco and presented reform proposals to the makhzen. This step angered Germany, who asserted that Morocco was independent and that its sultan had supreme power in the country. In 1906, Germany called a conference of the major European powers and the United States. The conference decided that Morocco's independence should be respected, that all countries should have equal trade rights with Morocco, and that France and Spain would have the right to set up a police force in Morocco.

In spite of the conference, Morocco still remained in a state of turmoil. When a French citizen was murdered in Marrakech, the French seized the opportunity to occupy the city. Other incidents pushed France into Rabat and Casablanca.

When Sultan Moulay Hafid came to power in 1908, he was unable to suppress local revolts. He asked for French military assistance, and the French immediately moved into Fez. Spain reacted by capturing the Moroccan towns of Larache and Alcazarquivir (Ksar-el-Kebir) on the Mediterranean coast and by strengthening positions throughout the northern part of the country. Germany reacted by sending a gunboat into the Bay of Agadir. On November 30, 1911, Germany and France came to an agreement: Germany would stay out of Morocco, and in turn France would stay out of the Congo, where Germany had strong interests.

THE FRENCH PROTECTORATE

The pressure on Morocco was too strong. On March 30, 1912, French Foreign Minister Eugene Regnault signed the Treaty of Fez with Sultan Moulay Hafid, setting up a French protectorate in Morocco that would last forty-three years—until independence in 1956. General Louis Lyautey was appointed resident general of the new protectorate. The treaty specified that the French protectorate would preserve the position and authority of the sultan and his government, maintain public order, modernize commerce and trade systems, and regulate Morocco's foreign relations.

The treaty also said that the city of Tangier, located at the head of the Strait of Gibraltar, would become an international zone. As a result, trade with the east would never be impeded by conflicts over who controlled the strait. Lastly, the treaty stated that Spanish interests would be protected.

In November another treaty established a Spanish protectorate in the north and in part of the desert. The city of Ifni on the Atlantic coast became a sovereign Spanish territory.

Although the sultan was supposed to be sovereign, he did not actually rule the country. The resident general did. But Lyautey loved Morocco and respected the Islam religion. Under Lyautey the French built up a strong modern economy. They introduced fruit, vegetables, and wine grapes to the country and mined some of the richest phosphate deposits in the world. They modernized the tax system and the roads and railroads and made Casablanca a great port.

In the 1920s, European-style cities with modern hygiene and sanitation facilities were built, away from the old Moroccan cities. But the average Moroccan was not affected by the modern advances in the country. It was all done for the advantage of the Europeans and rich Moroccans, not for the country itself. As Moroccans came to these cities to work, shantytowns called *bidonvilles* were set up near the cities, where these new immigrants lived in squalor while they worked at low-paying unskilled jobs.

Education for the children of the French colonists was the same as in

During the 1920s, shantytowns called bidonvilles *(above) were built near the cities as homes for the working Moroccans. These are being replaced by low-cost urban housing, such as the project under construction near Meknès (opposite).*

France. Only as the education system expanded were Moroccan children allowed to attend, too.

THE BERBERS REVOLT

The French used military force to gain control of the *bled as-siba,* but the fighting was bitter. The Berbers had fought and defeated so many peoples in the past that they were certain they could defeat the French. But the Berber stronghold finally began to break in 1920, when the great chief, Moha ou Hammou, died. Then the Middle Atlas surrendered to the French. In 1924 a warrior from the Rif named Abd-el-Krim attacked Fez with twenty thousand men. Though the Spanish and French had a combined army of more than four hundred thousand, it took them two years to defeat the leader of the Rif War. It took more than seven more years for the French to finally subdue the Anti-Atlas.

Resident general Lyautey did not like France's position in Morocco as protector

of the makhzen. He thought France should be in Morocco solely to preserve trade. The French government in Paris wanted direct rule over Morocco, and there was much pressure from all sides to get rid of Lyautey. In July of 1925, he was replaced, and direct rule followed quickly. The new resident general and his staff handled all legislation. The local officials, such as pashas and caids, remained, but now they all took orders from the French. Over the years, the power held by local officials degenerated to nothing.

THE NATIONALIST MOVEMENT

Educated Moroccans began to resent the total control of their country by the French. A religious reform movement known as the Salafiya began in the early 1920s at Karaouine University in Fez. Seeking to modernize Islam, the Salafiya opened schools that taught Arabic and Islam. Previously, the only schools had been French, and had not taught these subjects. The new schools showed that

Moroccans could modernize the country without French help.

Another movement was developed in 1925 by students at Rabat. Opposed to France's increased intervention in Morocco, they sought political independence. Soon they founded secret societies to make their feelings known. By 1927 these two movements had begun to merge, and the secret societies were springing up throughout the country.

In 1930 the French responded with the Berber *dahir* (decree). The French said that the dahir would modernize the legal system by taking power from the makhzen and giving it to the traditional Berber *djemaas,* or councils. Moroccans said that it was an attempt by France to gain control by dividing Morocco's Arab and Berber peoples. As a result of the dahir, there were many protests throughout the Muslim world. Moroccan nationalist leaders were arrested in demonstrations.

The protests and the subsequent arrests led to accelerated Moroccan nationalism. Most of the overt sentiment was shown outside the country, since the nationalist movement was strongest among Moroccan students studying in France or Spain.

In 1934 a committee of nationalist leaders known as CAM tried to obtain reforms. They wrote letters and newspaper editorials and sent petitions to the government. But the French rejected all their programs. After two years, CAM split into two factions. Muhammad Hassan Ouezzani and the traditionalists formed the Popular Movement. The rest of CAM, led by Allal al-Fassi, formed the National Party. The French wanted to eliminate the nationalist movement, so in 1937 they sent al-Fassi and Ouezzani into exile.

When World War II broke out, the Moroccan nationalist movements came together once again. Sultan Sidi Muhammad did not support France after it fell to Germany, but stayed with the Allies.

In 1943 Sultan Sidi Muhammad, President Franklin D. Roosevelt of the United States, and Prime Minister Winston Churchill of England held a conference at Casablanca. Roosevelt said that the United States would support the Moroccan people, so the Allies sent troops to fight in Morocco. Three hundred thousand Moroccans fought on the side of the Allies in North Africa, Italy, and France. In turn, the Allies showed support for the Moroccans by building air bases on Moroccan territory and sending soldiers to Morocco. The Moroccans had expected that the French would ease their control of Morocco when the Allies arrived. But this was not the case. The nationalist movement was still suppressed.

NATIONAL UNITY

During World War II the Moroccans who left their homeland to fight on the side of the Allies became aware that a wave of decolonization was spreading throughout the world. People at home were becoming disillusioned with the French protectorate. The people became

Government buildings in Rabat, the capital of Morocco.

united in the cause of self-government and there emerged a powerful national unity.

In January of 1944 the Istiglal (Independent Party) was formed by some long-time nationalist leaders, young urban intellectuals, and middle-class Moroccans. The Istiglal held a conference in Rabat at which they produced a manifesto asking for independence as well as political and social reforms. This was one of the first public demands for independence within Morocco. The sultan approved the entire manifesto, but the French approved only the political and social reforms. Istiglal rejected the French government's plans for reform and a few days later, eighteen Istiglal leaders were arrested. Immediately riots broke out against the French. Later, more nationalist parties were formed, including the Democratic Independence Party (PDI), which Ouezzani began when he returned from exile. Rather than prepare the Moroccans for eventual self-government, however, the French continued with their policy of governing through direct rule.

Resident general Erik Labonne, who came to Morocco after the war had ended, did attempt to introduce some reforms in 1946 to improve living standards and give Moroccans more voice in the government. But the sultan, who by this time was openly supporting the nationalists, was not satisfied with these reforms and refused to sign the dahirs. He wanted complete independence for Morocco.

In 1947 Sultan Sidi Muhammad made a journey to the free city of Tangier. He planned to speak out for cooperation between France and Morocco, but while he was away, a riot broke out in Casablanca. Angry that the French had fired on innocent Moroccans in Casablanca, the sultan instead spoke out for national unity and self-government in his speeches in Tangier. The Casablanca incident shattered all hopes for cooperation. The French reacted by replacing Labonne with a more conservative man, Alphonse Juin. As resident general, Juin attempted to tighten the French hold on Morocco by weakening the makhzen and discrediting the sultan.

Much tension ensued during the next few years. The French government proposed a number of reforms which the sultan repeatedly refused to sign. In 1950 the sultan went to Paris to discuss the growing crisis with the French government and to speak out for Moroccan self-government. But the sultan's suggestions were all ignored.

The Moroccans showed Sidi Muhammad great support when he returned from France, and even resident general Juin was becoming afraid of the sultan's power. A few months later Juin demanded that the sultan sign the dahirs originally proposed by Labonne. When the sultan again refused, the resident general threatened to depose him.

There were some Moroccans, however, who were pro-French. One of these was the pasha of Marrakech, Thami al-Glaoui.

In 1950 he attacked the sultan for supporting the nationalists. Immediately, the sultan threw him out of the palace. With a troop of dissident Berber tribes, al-Glaoui attacked Rabat and Fez. Finally, under this pressure, the sultan was forced to sign the dahirs, and many Istiglal leaders were subsequently arrested. The people were angered by these events and felt that the sultan had been insulted. The badly split nationalist parties united in their opposition to the French by forming a new party called the Moroccan National Front.

Two years later al-Glaoui, with his Berber troops and tanks, surrounded the palace at Rabat. Because the sultan was a symbol of Moroccan unity against the French, he was arrested and exiled to Madagascar. The French ordered the *ulema* (governing council) to choose a new sultan, and they selected Muhammad Moulay Ben Arafa. The exile of Sidi Muhammad ben Yussef did not quell the nationalist movement, as resident general Juin had hoped. Instead, it served only to outrage many Moroccans and terrorism broke out in opposition to the French.

The Islamic people of Morocco view their sultan as more than a political leader. He is also the religious leader, or *imam*. So when the new sultan abolished some Islam traditions and ceremonies connected with Sidi Muhammad ben Yussef the people became furious. Consequently, they did not respect Muhammad Moulay Ben Arafa as their sultan. Many refused to say prayers to him or even to pray at the mosques as the Islam religion required.

Support grew for the sultan in exile and the people became united in their demand that he be returned to Morocco.

By 1953 all of Istiglal's original leaders had been arrested or imprisoned. New, younger leaders, impatient for independence, arose in the party. Under these leaders, Moroccans began to boycott French cafes and cinemas and refused to buy European goods. In the next two years more than six thousand acts of terrorism occurred. Any Moroccan who continued to sell European goods soon became a victim of this terrorism. Hundreds were killed and many were wounded during this time. By 1955, the terrorist guerrillas were organized into an Army of Liberation, composed of about two thousand men.

The terrorism reached a peak on August 20, 1955, when Berber tribesmen from the Middle Atlas attacked the village of Oued-Zem, killing every Frenchman in the village. Also at about this time, Berbers in the Rif rebelled against the French. In the face of these pressures, France finally brought Sidi Muhammad ben Yussef back to Morocco. Sidi Muhammad Moulay Ben Arafa was deposed and negotiations for independence began immediately in Paris. On March 2, 1956, the French-Moroccan Agreement was signed, proclaiming Morocco an independent nation. On April 7 an agreement between Spain and Morocco was signed. Spain kept Melilla and Ceuta on the Mediterranean coast. In October of that year, Tangier was restored to Morocco.

Moroccan women rest in the shade outside a government building in Casablanca.

Morocco Today

After independence, Sidi Muhammad ben Yussef began to call himself King Muhammad V, because he felt that the title "sultan" was too closely related to the past. In a Royal Charter, the king declared that he advocated a democracy under a constitutional monarchy. He promised that there would be a constitution by 1962, and soon after independence he took steps in this direction by creating a consultative assembly and a cabinet. The cabinet was made up of nine Istiglals, six members of PDI (a more conservative group), and six independents.

PROBLEMS

The period immediately after independence was not an easy one for Morocco. Terrorism continued after independence because the radical nationalists wanted France out of Morocco completely. In 1956 most of the members of the Army of Liberation, which had been engaged in terrorism, joined the Royal Moroccan Army. However, there was still some terrorism near the Algerian border and it went on until 1958, when the last leaders of the original Army of Liberation were imprisoned.

There was more post-independence resistance from Berbers in the Rif and Middle Atlas. They felt that the new government was dominated by Arabs, and that not enough attention was paid to the Berbers. But by the beginning of 1959, Berber resistance had been put down by the government.

The government's greatest problem was to train the Moroccan people to run the army, the government offices, and the police force. For forty years, the French had run the country, and at independence the Moroccans were not prepared to take over. When the French government workers went on strike shortly after independence, government business stopped. Moroccan leaders then realized how important it was to *Moroccanize*—to replace French workers by Moroccan workers in all jobs. They also decided to *Arabize*—to use the Arabic language rather than the French as the official language of business and government.

Moroccanization came quickly. Only four years after independence, 72 percent of all governmental positions and half of all technical positions were held by Moroccans. Not all the new workers were qualified for the jobs they filled, however, and this caused even more problems.

POLITICAL PARTIES

Istiglal was the major political party after independence. Because it had done so much to attain independence, it was well-known throughout the country. There were other political parties, but they were not as well organized as Istiglal was. In

After independence, Moroccan leaders realized how important it was to fill governmental and technical positions with Moroccans. Below: Students train in an electronics workshop in Casablanca.

order to avoid a one-party system, the king included members of other parties in his cabinet. But by 1958, Istiglal virtually dominated the government.

At about that same time, splinter groups began to break away from Istiglal. Some Istiglal members had gone underground in the mountain areas to work with dissident Berbers. These rural Berbers formed the Popular Movement (MP) in 1958. In January of 1959 young, radical members of Istiglal split from the party to form the National Union of Popular Forces (UNFP). This leftist group advocated socialism (ownership by the government of all major means of production) and had enough influence to split the cabinet and make the workings of government come nearly to a halt. In May 1960, King Muhammad V assumed direct leadership of the government. He made himself premier and established a new cabinet with members from many political parties. Then he outlined a plan for making the government more democratic and in November appointed a council, made up mostly of Istiglals, to draft a constitution. This council did not complete its work for it broke up the following year at the death of the king.

THE CONSTITUTION

Moulay Hassan succeeded his father as premier and king in March of 1961. He immediately announced that he would follow his father's policies. The UNFP

King Hassan II.

refused to participate in Hassan's government because Hassan controlled it exclusively. The king did write a constitution, but without an elected council to advise him. Instead he sought the help of French advisers.

In December of 1962, the constitution was ready and the king presented it to the people of Morocco. A referendum was held so the people could vote on whether or not they wanted to accept this document. The palace conducted a powerful campaign for ratification of the constitution. Sound trucks traveled through the cities and countryside, their loudspeakers blaring support of ratification.

The campaign was carried on the radio, in newsreels, and on television. Several thousand TV receivers were set up throughout the countryside especially for this campaign.

Istiglal and other political parties supported the king's constitution, but the UNFP and the Moroccan Labor Union (UMT) were against it. Feeling that it should have been written by an elected council, the two groups tried to boycott the referendum. They were unsuccessful, mainly because they were unable to bring their campaign to TV and radio, which were owned and controlled by the government. The media were very influential: 95 percent of the people who voted in the referendum voted for ratification.

The new constitution set legal limits to the king's power for the first time in Moroccan history, but the king still had ultimate control. This form of government is called a democratic monarchy, and consists of three branches: an executive branch, with the king as the main figure; a judiciary branch; and a two-house Parliament, which makes laws.

STATE OF EMERGENCY

Problems were not over for the Moroccan government, particularly money problems. Food and clothing were getting more expensive. The Moroccan Labor Union, of which most workers were members, was demanding a 30 percent pay increase.

There were many splits in the existing political parties. In 1963 the UNFP fell apart after its leaders were arrested and tried on charges of plotting against the king. That same year the Front for the Defense of Constitutional Institutions (FDIC) was formed; it was a *royalist* party, loyal to the king. The following year, liberals broke away from the FDIC, forming the Socialist Democratic Party (PSD). PSD was not, however, a political party; it was a group formed to promote free enterprise. By 1965 the political situation had become so confusing that the public had lost confidence in almost all the parties.

In 1965, the king decreed that only a few select people would be able to get a complete education. Most of the people would have to be content with just a few years of school; consequently, it would be harder for them to get good jobs. In Casablanca students demonstrated against this decree. The demonstrations were peaceful until idle crowds joined the students. Then rioting, which lasted three days, broke out. Most of the rioters were from Casablanca's slums. The situation grew even more tense as riots developed elsewhere in the country.

The riots did not occur only as a result of the education decree. The rioters also wanted the king to free some people who had been put in jail because their beliefs were thought to be against the government. To help end the riots, the king freed some of these political prisoners. Although this helped relieve some of the tension, it

A government building in Casablanca.

did not solve the problem. So the king then met with leaders of all the political parties in an attempt to form a stronger government. He even accepted some of the opposition's demands. But nothing seemed to alleviate the problem, and on June 8, 1965, the king declared a state of emergency in Morocco. (The Moroccan government officially called it a "state of exception.")

According to the 1962 constitution, during a state of emergency the king assumes all legislative and executive powers and names a new government not based on political parties. The king did just that, and he also formed three new ministries connected with economic problems.

The state of emergency lasted for five years, and in July of 1970 a new constitution was submitted to a public referendum. The constitution was approved and elections were held. Istiglal and the UNFP, who had lost power during the state of emergency, joined together as the National Front to boycott the elections. They claimed that the constitution was too restrictive. But the elections took place in spite of their boycott, ending the state of exception.

MOROCCO

PROVINCES

THE GOVERNMENT

The constitution proclaims that Morocco is a sovereign Muslim state. The people look up to the king not only as the leader of the state but also as their *imam,* or religious leader. This is important in maintaining his power and authority. Much power is concentrated in the king, and the constitution does not provide a way for other branches of the government, such as Parliament (the legislature) and the supreme court, to check up on the king. Thus, the king is an extremely strong figure.

The king appoints the prime minister (head of government) and other ministers. There are two other branches of government. One is the judicial, consisting of a supreme court, regional courts, and three courts of appeal. Supreme court judges are appointed by the king. The other is the legislature, called Parliament. Parliament is composed of 240 members with six-year terms. Ninety members are elected directly by the people and 150 are elected by special-interest groups. The king can dissolve Parliament whenever he wants to, but if he does, new elections must be held within forty days.

The constitution divides Morocco into nineteen provinces and two prefectures (Rabat and Casablanca). Each of these is headed by a governor appointed by the king.

EDUCATION

Traditionally, education in Morocco was oriented toward religion. Children recited the *Koran* for a teacher at the local mosque for a few years. Only the wealthy children received further education at a *medersa,* an advanced religious school.

When Morocco was divided into French and Spanish protectorates, schools run by these governments taught primarily French and Spanish children. The French did not permit any Moroccan children to attend their schools, but some were allowed to attend the Spanish schools. In 1938, people interested in Moroccan independence started private schools taught in Arabic for Moroccan children. About 1940, Moroccan children were finally allowed to attend European schools, but not many went, since the cost was too high for most Moroccans. In 1944 French schools in Morocco began to teach Arabic as a subject.

At independence in 1956, only 10 percent of all Moroccan children had ever been to school. Most of these were children of Moroccan elite. The new government tried to expand the education system rapidly, but it was difficult to do; there was a lack of buildings, overcrowded rooms, and underqualified teachers. Because there were twice as many students as there were seats and rooms for them, rooms in other buildings were borrowed. Teachers were badly needed—so badly that people with only primary-school educations (the equivalent of sixth grade) sometimes had to teach primary school. In 1961 a program called Operation Schools began, in which local people contributed materials and labor in order to build more schools for their children.

The new government also wanted to teach school in Arabic instead of French, a foreign language. A program of Arabization of the schools was immediately begun, but it was hard to find mathematics and science textbooks in Arabic and to teach advanced subjects in Arabic.

Today, children in Morocco go to primary school from ages seven through twelve. School lasts for thirty hours a week, about as long as in the United States. Three hours a day are spent at a mosque, where children learn Islamic subjects. The rest of the time is spent on such subjects as arithmetic, geometry, Moroccan history, geography, physical education, religion, Arabic, and French. In rural areas farming is also taught.

Still, nearly two thirds of the children in Morocco drop out of primary school. If a child finishes primary school and passes final exams, he can continue on to secondary school. If he fails the exams, he can still attend vocational classes in agriculture, handicrafts, or home economics.

A secondary school student can take one or two cycles. Each cycle lasts four years. In the first cycle, the student takes many different subjects, but a student in the second cycle specializes either in traditional Arabic subjects or in modern subjects.

Few students who qualify for secondary school finish it, and of those who do only a few go to college. About 20 percent of these study abroad, mostly in Europe. The rest go to one of Morocco's few universities, such as Karaouine University at Fez or the University of Rabat. People come from all over the world to attend Morocco's Karaouine University. The oldest university in North Africa, it was started in 859 A.D. as a religious university. In the early 1960s, Karaouine University was reorganized into a national university with three branches, one each

Through the United Nations World Food Program, food is being distributed at this boys' school in Tétouan and at many other schools in Morocco.

The University of Karaouine has three branches, one each at Fez, Marrakech, and Tétouan. Right: A Moroccan studies at the Library of Marrakech.

at Fez, Marrakech, and Tétouan. It is still a religious university. The University of Rabat was begun in 1957. Also called Muhammad V University, it is a secular (not religious) university.

Government agencies give courses to people who cannot attend school. Women's Centers of Rural Development (CFER) teach household skills and reading to about fifteen thousand women each year. In 1961 a program was set up by the government to teach basic school skills such as reading, writing, and arithmetic to people who never attended or did not finish primary school.

HEALTH

In rural areas, doctors with modern medical techniques are slowly taking the place of medicine men with magical cures. But water pollution and sanitation are still problems. In the north water often has too many minerals in it. Rivers and wells throughout the country are usually polluted, but in some areas even these dry up in the summer. In the cities and large towns, the reservoirs usually hold enough water for the people all year. Water is piped from the reservoir to houses. But in villages, good water must be obtained

At independence, the government began a policy of free medical care and health education for all Moroccans. Right: Good nutrition practices are taught at the Health Circumscription of Yacoub el-Mansour Mother and Child Health Program. Below: Patients wait at the dispensary of the Health Circumscription.

from street fountains or pumps or brought in goatskin containers by water carriers.

There is almost no modern sanitation except in the new parts of the cities. In the villages, wastes are often dumped into the only water supply. In the city, wastes are dumped into open ditches, into the street, or into pits in the courtyards, where the wastes are collected and sold for fertilizer.

Because of the poor sanitation, contagious diseases are prevalent in Morocco. Flies, mosquitoes, lice, fleas, ticks, and water snails all carry contagious diseases. Malaria, typhoid, bilharzia, dysentery, tuberculosis, and venereal disease are also common. People throughout Morocco receive inoculations for these diseases.

Another serious problem in Morocco is blindness. About 60 percent of all Moroccans have something wrong with their eyes. One of the biggest causes of eye problems is trachoma, a disease which can cause blindness if not treated. Programs are being carried out throughout the country to combat trachoma.

At independence, the government began a policy of free medical care and health education for all Moroccans. Private medical care is also available.

The country is in need of all kinds of medical people: doctors, dentists, pharmacists, nurses, and midwives. At independence, most medical personnel in Morocco were French. But more and more Moroccans are entering this profession, because the government pays for their schooling. Medical schools are located at Casablanca and Rabat, and many Moroccans study medicine abroad. The State School of Nursing and Social Workers at Casablanca trains nurses. There are three medical research institutes in Morocco: Pasteur Institutes in Casablanca and Rabat (which conduct general research and make serums) and the Institute of Hygiene at Rabat (which conducts lab studies).

Natural Treasures

PLANTS

Many parts of the Rif are covered with scrubby, low bushes where erosion has ravaged the land. But along the many riverbeds grow pines, evergreens, and walnut trees, along with thickets of cane. Cedar forests extend through the Rif and the Atlas, completely covering the highest peaks. To the west, in the plains and plateaus, grow lilies and dwarf palms, and grasses such as alfalfa and esparto. The *callito* (eucalyptus) is used throughout the country as a shade tree. Argan forests span southern Morocco and date palms flourish in the desert oases. Rows of fragrant furze line mile after mile of the main roads of Morocco.

Olives are plentiful everywhere in Morocco, especially in gardens, where the fragrant aroma of herbs and flowers fills the air. Yellow jasmine, vivid geraniums, reddish-orange poppies, and pink carnations brighten up the patios of the many white houses in the cities. Herbs are abundant throughout the country; there are basil, *kamoun* (cumin), *oosbour* (coriander), *mrededouch* (marjoram), and *nana* (mint). These herbs have uses other than as spices for cooking; some are used as medicines and others are used to keep away pesty mosquitoes.

Date palms flourish throughout Morocco, especially in the desert oases.

Olives are plentiful in Morocco. These Moroccan boys are using a masra *(stone mill) to extract oil from olives.*

ANIMALS

Small animals are abundant in Morocco. Along with hares and porcupines, rabbits scurry through the grasses, often fleeing from ferrets. This domesticated albino polecat is related to the skunk and is used by Berbers to hunt rabbits. Jackals and foxes prowl remote villages at night, hunting domestic sheep and goats. People whose livelihood depends on their herds must protect their sheep and goats very carefully from these predators.

The hedgehog also comes out after dark to search for insects. When threatened, the hedgehog rolls its hairy, spiny body into a ball. Out in the fields, the strange laugh of the striped hyena pierces the night as this animal scavenges for food.

High in the Atlas, fierce mountain cats and wild boar roam the land. Because the wild boar damages cultivated land, it is hunted by the Berbers, who sell the boar hides and use the tusks for religious rituals. In one part of the Atlas, near Chaouen, the Barbary ape can be found.

Interesting fish are plentiful in Morocco's coastal waters. Left: Fishing boats at the port of Tangier.

Birds such as ravens, cowbirds, sparrows, and hoopoes are found everywhere in Morocco. The hoopoe, with its slender bill that curves downward, is an important bird to Rif Berbers; they use its blood for magical preparations. Snipe, duck, quail, and partridge live in a tourist reserve.

Some poisonous snakes are found in southern Morocco, including vipers, puff adders, and Egyptian cobras.

Morocco has many small streams and rivers, and fish are plentiful there. The streams in the interior are full of brook, brown, and rainbow trout, black bass, pike, and perch. Many people like to fish in these waters, but they need a fishing license to do so. Interesting fish are plentiful in Morocco's coastal waters. Morocco's largest fish, the merou, is found off the Mediterranean coast. In the Atlantic are large rays, conger eels, bluefish, bonito (a kind of tuna), and sea bass. Underwater fishing is popular on the Moroccan coast, and clubs have been formed for this purpose in six of Morocco's coastal cities.

The People Live in Morocco

ARABIZATION

In the seventh century, the first Arabs came to Morocco. But they had little effect on the country's inhabitants until the eleventh century, when nomadic Bedouins began to travel throughout Morocco, spreading the Islamic religion and the Arabic language. They converted most of the people in the plains to their religion, but did not reach the mountain Berbers for a few more centuries. The Berbers slowly began to speak Arabic, the sacred language of their new religion. As more Arabization occurred, Arabs began marrying into Berber families. Today many people do not know whether their ancestors are Arab or Berber or both.

Some Arab nomads still live in the eastern plateaus of the country, especially in Ouled al-Hadj and Beni-Guil. Often these nomads establish close relations with a village near their travel route which raises and stores cereals and fruits for them.

Today more than fifteen thousand people live in Morocco; most of them are Arab Berbers. Other nationalities compose a distinct minority. About two hundred thousand Europeans live in the country. Sixty percent of them are French, 30 percent are Spanish, and the rest are Italian, Portuguese, and other nationalities. Most Europeans live in the larger cities of Morocco and work in either business or the professions.

These Berber women are from a small village in the western Rif.

BERBERS

There are about two hundred Berber groups in Morocco; the name of each group is the name of a supposed common ancestor or a place important to the group. In isolated rural regions, each group has a specific symbol, such as the color of their *djellabas* (robes), the shape of their shoes, or the design on their pottery.

The people of some of these groups still cluster together in certain rural areas. The Rhmara are found in the coastal hills of the Rif. An ancestral story tells that these Berbers are descendants of an immigrant schoolteacher's nine sons.

Sanhaja Berbers are found in the western Rif and the High Atlas. Historians believe the Sanhaja was the tribe that set out in the third century A.D. to conquer the Sahara. Both the Rhmara and the Sanhaja live with their extended families in clusters of ten to fifty houses. Men take care of the grain, vegetables, and fruit, while women tend the cattle and goats.

In the eastern Rif live Rifian Berbers. They grow wheat and raise sheep and cattle. These Berbers wear their turbans in a distinctive way: across their head, two fingers above the eyebrow.

Imaziren Berbers live in the High Atlas. Their villages were once fortresses against attackers. The high walls of these villages protect clusters of red-earth buildings. The people grow cereals near the villages and raise cattle and sheep in a nearby pasture. At the end of the harvest season, they move to a new pasture far from their village, where they live in tents throughout that season.

In the desert oases live the Zenata Berbers. Traditionally they were nomad horsemen, once the most feared cavalrymen in the Islamic armies.

Most rural Berbers have not changed much over the centuries. Many are still peasants or shepherds, unconcerned with the development of the modern world. They still cling to their traditional ways of working and thinking. But other Berbers have become educated, moved to the cities, gotten jobs, and lost touch with their ethnic groups. These Berbers have become a part of the modern, urban world. They have become increasingly Westernized through radio, newspapers, and close contact with Europeans.

LANGUAGE

Almost all the people in Morocco speak more than one language. About three fourths of the people speak Arabic (the national language) as their first language. Some rural Berbers speak Berber as a main language, though they use Arabic in the marketplace. Many Moroccans also speak French or Spanish.

The Arabic language can be spoken or written in two ways, which are actually quite similar. Classical Arabic is the more formal, and is the language of government, business, and religion. It is more often written than spoken. Modern Arabic is the language of the people, spoken within the family and on the streets.

A Berber village in the western Rif.

WAY OF LIFE

The traditional way of life revolved around the extended family, which lived and worked as a unit. Around a central area were the family's many buildings or tents. Each married couple had its own place to sleep, but food and wealth were communally owned. Women stayed at home cooking, weaving, and caring for the children, while the men worked in the fields or went to market. When the headman of the village died, the family often broke up into smaller units, each starting a new village nearby.

In many parts of Morocco, people still follow this traditional way of life. But where Western-style education has been introduced, the extended family is not as strong. People who have been to school have learned that the way of their ancestors is not the only way and that they do not need to depend so strongly on their families. Thus, many of them have left their home villages and gone to the cities for work.

There are about two hundred Berber groups in Morocco, each with its own customs or symbols. Opposite page, top left: Berber girls from the High Atlas; top right: A young Berber from the pre-Sahara; bottom left: A Berber girl sits in front of an Arab tent; bottom right: A Berber woman from northern Morocco. On this page, right: Berber girls from the Rif in festival costumes; below: This Berber dance company performs the music from their tribe.

OFFICE NATIONAL MAROCAIN DU TOURISME

UNITED NATIONS

The role of women is changing in Morocco, especially in the cities. Here girls are marching in an athletic tournament.

Muslims who live in the cities are generally more Westernized than those in rural areas. But even in the cities, there is no socializing between men and women, except in more Westernized households. Even there, women usually socialize with men only when Europeans are present. Most Muslim women socialize with other women at the public bath, at a nearby shrine, or at the house of a relative, but never outdoors in public. Muslim men socialize with each other at their shops, at mosques, at the marketplace, or at cafes. Men spend more leisure time at cafes than

they do at home, where they usually go only to eat or sleep.

For a long time, Muslim women always wore veils, but this tradition is slowly ending in the cities. Since Moroccan independence, many women have dropped their veils, and today a variety of styles can be seen. Some women wear no veil, some drape one around their chin, and others remain covered to their eyes.

The role of the woman has become an important topic in Morocco, especially among the educated. Though most Muslim women are still secluded, many are now

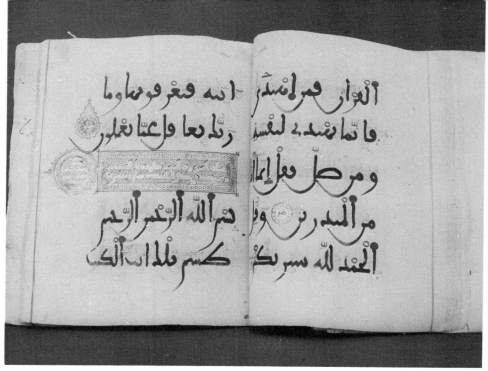

The Koran is the holy book of the Islam religion.

out of the veil and the house, working. The government says that women should take a more active role in life outside the home, but many Muslim men are afraid that the home will suffer if their wives leave it to work.

RELIGION

Ninety-eight percent of the people in Morocco follow Islam, the national religion. People who follow this religion are called Muslims, or Moslems. The founder of Islam was Muhammad (also spelled Mohammed), born in Mecca in the year 570. After receiving a message from the angel Gabriel, he started to preach his religion. But he was forced to flee the city in 622. Muhammad's flight from Mecca is called the *hejira*, and 622 on the Christian calendar is the first year of the Muslim calendar. Muhammad converted many people to his new religion, which eventually controlled all of Arabia.

When Muhammad died, his followers collected his words, which they considered divinely revealed, into a book called the *Koran*. This is the Islamic holy book. His followers also put together a second book, called the *Hadiths*, which included more of Muhammad's words and examples of his personal behavior that became rules of life for Muslims. These two books are the basis of the Muslim way of life.

All Muslims try to follow the main tenets of the Islam religion, called the Five Pillars. The first is a creed called the *shahadah:* "There is no God but Allah, and Muhammad is his Prophet." Muslims recite this creed before all important prayers. The second tenet states that Muslims must pray five times a day. Third, they must give alms to the poor. Fourth, Muslims must fast during the month of *Ramadan* (third month of the lunar calendar). Fifth, Muslims should try to make the *hadj,* or pilgrimage to Mecca, which is the birthplace of Muhammad and the holy city of the Islamic religion. After a person has made this pilgrimage, he can add the title "al-Hadj" before his name.

During Ramadan, all Muslims fast, except the sick, soldiers, and travelers. These do their fasting when they are able. No one eats or smokes from dawn to dusk. At sundown, people are already seated at tables, spoons in their hands, around a large bowl of steaming hot *harira,* a soup made of eggs, meat chunks, and chickpeas. As soon as the signal for sundown has been given (whether it is cannon shots in the cities or the cry of the muezzin atop a mosque in the villages), everyone gulps down his harira. In remote areas, where there is no official signal to end the day, people use an age-old test. When they are no longer able to distinguish a white thread from a black thread, it is dusk.

After dark, the streets come alive. Everyone is awake, for an extra prayer is said at night during the month of Ramadan. People wait at home for prayer time or go to the mosque.

Muslims believe in *baraka,* a holiness or blessed virtue that Allah gives to special people, or saints. People who possess baraka can do supernatural things, such as make themselves invisible, change shapes, heal the sick, and foresee the future. Other people can get baraka from contact with a saint, by engaging in a *jihad* (holy war), or through extreme piety and devotion; people who obtain baraka in these ways are called *marabouts.* Muslims believe that a person's baraka increases when he dies. Thus, tombs of saints and marabouts are worshipped.

Many Muslims still believe in traditional superstitions. One of these is *chu-ba,* the evil eye: a glance or a look from people who possess the chu-ba can cause an evil or deadly spell. To find out if someone has put the evil eye on them, Muslims use a piece of translucent stone. The stone is put in a fire until it is hot. If an eye appears on it, the person knows that the curse of the evil eye is on him.

There are a number of remedies to counteract the evil eye and other spells. These remedies include incantations, "magical colors" such as yellow, blue, or red, and the number five. People often inscribe the number five or sacred passages from the Koran in an amulet to protect them from evil. Berber women sometimes tattoo the number five on their faces.

The People Work in Morocco

Nations try to maintain a *balance of trade*; that is, they want the value of their imports to be roughly equivalent to that of their exports. Morocco has what is called an unfavorable balance of trade. It imports more goods than it exports: In 1970 its imports totaled $632 million and exports only $492 million. Most of Morocco's international trade is with France, but the USSR and West Germany are also important trade partners. Morocco's main exports are cork, canned fish, and phosphates, and such agricultural products as citrus fruits, vegetables, and wine.

AGRICULTURE

The people in Morocco have traditionally lived off their own crops and livestock, trading what they didn't need with people in their own or a nearby village.

During the French protectorate, the French introduced fruits, vegetables, and wine grapes to Morocco for commercial production and export to other countries. Even today, 70 percent of the people in Morocco earn their living from agriculture.

Some farmers, especially in rural areas, grow crops and raise livestock simply to live on; these people are called *subsistence farmers*. Their methods of agriculture are extremely primitive, for modern technology has not yet reached them. Other Moroccan farmers are *truck farmers;* they grow products (mostly vegetables) which they sell in the marketplace.

Many varieties of crops are grown in Morocco. Grains such as sorghum, millet, and oats, and seeds such as peas, beans, lentils, and chick-peas are grown

Many Moroccan farms are large, with modern machinery and excellent livestock.

primarily for farmers to feed their families. Nuts, especially almonds, also flourish here. Olives, flaxseed, sunflower seeds, and castor beans are cultivated for their oils. Vast groves of citrus fruits, mainly oranges, abound in the coastal plains. Also, there are miles of grape vineyards in Morocco. Most of the wine is exported because not many Moroccans drink wine. Alcohol is forbidden by the Islamic religion.

Livestock are plentiful in Morocco, especially in the mountain areas. Sheep, goats, and cattle are kept for meat and milk. The wool from sheep and goats is used by local crafts people. There are also many work animals, including camels, mules, donkeys, and horses.

LAND HOLDINGS

There are four ways land can be owned in Morocco. *Makhzen* land is owned by the government. Land donated to religious foundations is *habous* land; it is rented to groups or individuals. Other land is owned communally by a tribe; communal councils, or *djemaas*, administer this land. *Melk* land is privately owned. The most common privately owned farm is the *khammessatt*. Here the landowner supplies land, seed, tools, clothing, and food to a sharecropper. The sharecropper works the land and receives part of the crop (usually one fifth). The landowner gets the rest of the crop. After independence, fifty thousand acres of land were distributed to landless peasants.

INDUSTRY

There is not much industry in Morocco. Most of it is centered in Casablanca, because it is the main port. Before World War II, the only industry in Morocco was food processing. The first food-processing plant made flour and cereals. Today there are a few sugar refineries, but most sugar is imported. Beer and carbonated beverages have been produced since 1919.

Fish canning, a very big industry, began in 1925 at Mohammedia. This industry has expanded rapidly ever since. The sardine, tuna, and anchovy found in the Atlantic Ocean are now canned at various port cities and then exported.

There is also a substantial textile industry in Morocco. Cotton, wool, yarn, and cloth fibers are imported and woven in Morocco. Sisal and hemp are made into bags, twine, and rope.

Morocco's many forests provide wood for the country's five pulp and paper mills. Four of these use eucalyptus wood and alfalfa grass, both of which are abundant in the country. The huge cork industry is owned by the government, and much cork is exported.

Morocco provides 40 percent of the world's phosphates. Until 1965 all these phosphates were exported raw. Now phosphates are processed at the Safi chemical complex into fertilizer, sulfuric acid, phosphoric acid, and superphosphoric acid (later made into ammonia).

It is hard for Morocco to expand its industry for three major reasons. First, the

Larache is one of the main tuna fishing and canning ports of Morocco.

only available energy is hydroelectric (water power), which is expensive. Second, there is a lack of technical and administrative people. And lastly, because Moroccans have little money, they have little buying power, so there is almost no market for industrial products.

TRANSPORTATION

When the protectorate was established in 1912, there were almost no roads in Morocco, except near the large cities. Roads weren't needed in the rural areas, since no one thought of traveling much farther than the distance between the home and the market. The French built roads so they could more easily administer their government. Today the road system is well developed except in the north (the former Spanish protectorate) and in remote areas. In fact, Morocco's highway system is the best in Africa. Many gas stations and vehicle repair shops are scattered throughout the country. The only area of low-quality roads is in the mountains, where there are only rough trails and dirt roads. These become impassable in bad weather, making it hard to modernize trade in the mountain areas.

There are taxis in the cities and towns. A *petit-taxi* costs one dirham (about U.S. $.20) for a trip anywhere in the city. There is good bus service throughout the country. The *Compagnie des Transports du Maroc* (CTM), the biggest bus company, is run by the Moroccan Auxiliary Transport Company.

Morocco's railroad was built during the protectorate by privately owned foreign companies. In 1936 the government took it over. The main line runs from Marrakech to Oujda through Casablanca, Rabat, Fez, and Meknès. It branches out to Tangier, Youssoufia, Safi, the mines near the Zem River, and to other railroads south of Oujda. There are about twelve hundred miles of railroad; about four hundred miles of track are electrified and the rest use diesel locomotives.

Morocco has six large ports on the Atlantic Ocean: Casablanca, Safi, Kenitra, Mohammedia, Tangier, and Agadir. The port of Casablanca is the third-largest port in all of Africa. Two thirds of Morocco's freight is shipped from here—mostly phosphates. The port of Mohammedia imports mostly petroleum. Kenitra's port, ten miles from the Sebou River, is a naval base that imports petroleum and exports citrus and vegetables grown on the nearby Rharb Plain.

There is good bus service throughout Morocco. Here villagers board a bus in Sefrou, near Fez.

The port of Tangier is the southern terminus of the ferry across the Strait of Gibraltar. The ferries carry many passengers, but not much freight. Car ferries from Tangier and Sebta in Morocco to Malaga and Algeurasin in Spain travel ten miles across the Strait of Gibraltar.

Air France and twelve other airlines fly to Morocco. There are airports in Rabat-Salé, Casablanca-Anfa, Agadir, Marrakech, Tangier, and Al Hoceima. All airports were originally built for military purposes by France, Spain, and the United States. Later they were converted to commercial use. The national airlines is Royal Air Maroc, owned jointly by Air France and the Moroccan government.

COMMUNICATIONS

The most important communication medium in Morocco is word of mouth. News can spread through the country with incredible speed, just by one person telling another. Although the government attempted to stop the news of the 1965 Casablanca riots from spreading, the news had reached every marketplace within only a few hours. This system has its drawbacks because false rumors can spread very rapidly. But the people seem to trust information they receive from friends more than information received from newspapers, radio, or television.

Print media (mostly newspapers) reach only about one third as many people as does radio, but these people are generally the more influential people of the country. Compared to the press in other countries, Morocco's press is controlled fairly tightly by the government. Yet the press has less government control than any other medium. The government does not tell the press what to print but it has the power to suspend the publication of any paper. Thus, newspapers with strong leanings toward a particular political viewpoint are very careful in what they print for fear of being closed.

Most of Morocco's larger newspapers were started during the protectorate by private French or Spanish companies. In 1965 there were nine daily newspapers: *Al Anbaa* (the official government paper), two Istiglal (political) papers, one UNFP (political) paper, and five privately owned papers. *La Petit Marocain* (French) and *España* (Spanish) were the most popular private papers, each with a circulation of more than forty thousand.

Several foreign papers are also published in Morocco: *Jeune Afrique*, the *New York Times* European edition, the Paris *Herald-Tribune,* and periodicals from the Middle East.

All broadcasting is controlled by the government, which used radio to gain support for the constitutional referendums. The government radio, called Radio Maroc, broadcasts mostly from Rabat. There are three networks: one in Arabic, one in French and Spanish, and a third in three Berber dialects. Not all parts of Morocco get good radio reception. The mountains often block it. Radio Maroc broadcasts on a shortwave band to reach remote southern Morocco and the rest of Africa and the Middle East.

Almost every house has a radio and radios in cafes and markets are played all day long. The people often listen to foreign radio programs such as Radio Cairo, the BBC (from England), Radio Paris, Radio Algiers, and Mauritanian radio. The United States' Voice of America broadcasts in Arabic, but it is not as popular as British or French radio.

Television was introduced in 1962. Moroccan television programs originate in Rabat, Marrakech, and Casablanca. Many programs shown on Moroccan television come from France and the United States.

Most movie theaters are owned by Europeans. Movies are popular—mostly light entertainment such as mysteries, American westerns, and French comedies. The Moroccan Motion Picture Center (CCM) is a government agency that makes documentary films.

Telephone, telegraph, and postal services are all government-owned and operated. There are cables to Algeria, West Africa, and Europe.

These Moroccan farmers are watching television for the first time in their lives.

MEDIA ADVISORS INTERNATIONAL, INC.

The beautiful Rif mountains stretch across northern Morocco. The villages in the Rif reflect the many cultures that have influenced the Berbers over the centuries.

The Enchantment of Morocco

Over the centuries, Morocco's Berbers have been influenced by people of other cultures—the Romans and their great empire, the Vandals and Byzantines of the north, the Arabs and their Islamic religion, the Portuguese traders, and most recently the Spanish and French. Morocco's history is rich with overthrown dynasties and conquerors. But the Berbers fought them all, retaining much of their own culture. Morocco is a composite of all these cultures, and different parts of the country reflect different influences.

THE RIF

The savagely beautiful Rif mountains stretch 220 miles across northern Morocco. At each end of the range is a Mediterranean coastal town that still belongs to Spain—Melilla in the east and Ceuta in the west. Between these towns, many islands are visible from the steep and rugged coastline.

Caught in a valley between the sea and the mountains, the people of the Rif have always been isolated from the rest of Morocco. They speak a Berber dialect called Tarrifit. Ruled by the Spanish protectorate for many years, the influence that is most prominent here is that of the Andalusian Moors, who controlled Spain hundreds of years ago.

Melilla is at the eastern end of the Rif mountains, on a peninsula that reaches twenty-five miles out into the Mediterranean Sea. Melilla is called *Tamlilt* in Berber, meaning "The White." Its population is completely Spanish.

Almost a hundred miles west, on the end of a bay, is the little port of Al Hoceima. The port harbors a fleet of fishing boats. At night the clear coastal waters are dotted with lights from *lamparos*, big lanterns that are mounted on the boats. The fish are stunned by the bright light and the men can just scoop them from the water.

With many dangerously sharp turns, the road to the west follows the high ridge of the cedar and pine-forested Rif mountains. High peaks tower into the sky, and deep below in the valleys are blue lakes.

About a hundred miles west of Al Hoceima is Tétouan, with a population of 100,000. The city was founded in the early fourteenth century by a Merinid sultan. For centuries Berbers and Spanish fought for the city. In the early nineteenth century, it became the capital of the Spanish protectorate. At one time Tétouan sheltered Mediterranean pirates who arrived via the nearby Martil River.

The road to the north from Tétouan gradually descends to sea level at the town of Ceuta, the western end of the Rif. Ceuta is on a tiny peninsula, only fifteen miles across the strait from Gibraltar, Spain. With a population that is 90 percent Spanish, Ceuta, too, is Andalusian in character.

THE CITY OF THE STRAIT

Located on the Strait of Gibraltar, Tangier is often called the "City of the Strait." Both the strait and the city itself have long historical importance. Captured by the Portuguese in 1471, Tangier became Spanish under Philip II. By 1640 it was under the Portuguese again, when it was given to a Portuguese princess as a dowry for her marriage to Charles II of England. But the British Parliament could not afford to defend it, and British soldiers evacuated the city in 1684. As they left, they destroyed the citadel and harbor. Tangier came under Moroccan rule for the next two hundred years.

The Strait of Gibraltar has always been important to the people of the Mediterranean as their only link to the Atlantic Ocean. With the opening of the Suez Canal in 1869, however, the strait became even more important. Making the Mediterranean more accessible to the rest of the world, the Strait of Gibraltar soon became part of an important trade route to the Middle East.

Because of the value of the strait, in 1912 Tangier was made an independent international zone so that possibly hostile countries would be discouraged from capturing the city and closing off the strait. As an international port, Tangier gained a reputation for intrigue. At Moroccan independence, it was given to the government of Morocco.

THE RHARB PLAIN

Heading south from Tangier the land is at first slightly hilly, but soon becomes completely flat. This is the Rharb Plain, a mostly fertile area marked with historic towns. Thirty miles south of Tangier on the Atlantic Ocean is Asilah, a town enclosed in a wall with only two gates. There

A farmer plows his fields on the Rharb Plain.

are miles of beautiful sandy beaches here. But Asilah's main attraction is the castle of the bandit Raisuli.

The next town south is the little port of Larache. A very ancient settlement, Larache was once a Phoenician trading post called Lix; the Romans took it over and called it Lixus. Ancient ruins can still be seen here.

The road south to Kenitra continues through an exceptionally fertile area. Cork forests, groves of orange and olive trees, rice paddies, and wheat fields all line the road. The rich soil of this plain is carried from the Atlas Mountains by the Sebou River, Morocco's second-largest river.

The city of Kenitra lies in the Sebou Valley. Originally called Port Lyautey, Kenitra was founded by Marshal Louis Lyautey, the French resident general, in 1913. The port was built around a *casbah*, a walled city. Local produce makes up most of the shipments through this port.

THE REPUBLIC OF THE TWO SHORES

On the Atlantic coast, about 250 miles south of Tangier, is the mouth of the Bou Regrez River. The city of Salé, founded in the eleventh century, is located on the river's north side. In 1260, Salé was sacked by Spaniards during *Aid Seghir*, the celebration ending the Ramadan fast month. After the sacking, fortifications, which still stand, were built.

In 1627, Salé and its southern neighbor, Rabat, became an independent republic known as The Republic of the Two Shores. The republic was a base for pirates, who attacked ships in the Atlantic, taking booty and captives. The wealthy they held for ransom; the poor they sold as slaves. But the republic lasted only fourteen years; internal strife and British attacks brought it to an end in 1641.

Rabat began as a Roman settlement. Ruins of the original Roman area, which is now called Chellah, still remain. The building of the city of Rabat was begun in 1150 by the first Almohad sultan. His son and grandson built the town as a military base, calling it Ribat El Fath ("The Camp of Victory"). Pink mud ramparts were

Often called "The White City," Rabat is a modern town with palm-lined boulevards.

MICHAEL ROBERTS

built around the city and a casbah was constructed on the mouth of the river. A mosque was also built whose minaret, the Hassan Tower, has walls eight feet thick.

But Rabat was still only a small town in 1913, when it was made the capital. Today Rabat is Morocco's second-largest city, with a population of 266,000. Often called "The White City" because of its many white villas, Rabat is a modern town with palm-lined boulevards and colorful public gardens. As the capital of Morocco, all the government ministries, foreign embassies, plus the king's residence are here.

THE HEART OF MOROCCO

On a plateau about a hundred miles east of Rabat lies the city of Meknès. It was founded in the tenth century by the Meknassa Berbers, who called it Meknès es Zeitoun, or "Meknès among the Olives." It became the capital of Morocco in 1673 under Moulay Ismail, who built a huge, fortified palace there, complete with gardens, stables, barracks, dungeons, and storerooms. This palace is now mostly in ruins.

Forty miles east of Meknès is Fez. This city is surrounded by yellow mud ramparts, which enclose a maze of rooftops, towers, and streets. In the background the green hills of the Middle Atlas fade into distant purple mountains.

Fez is considered the "heart of Morocco." Any invader from the west had to conquer Fez in order to pass through the nearby Taza Gap in the mountains; any invader from the east had to capture Fez in order to continue westward. The oldest of Morocco's imperial cities, Fez was founded about 800 by an Arab prince. In the thirteenth and fourteenth centuries, Fez was capital of the vast Merinid empire and became the intellectual center of the world. Scholars traveled from Europe and the Middle East to Fez's famed Karaouine University.

This university was begun in 859 when a pious lady named Fatima pledged sixty ounces of silver to start construction of a mosque. Wealthy sultans built schools around it. Every consecutive dynasty added something to the university or mosque. The pulpit was built in the eleventh century, the large bell came from Spain in the twelfth century, and the library door was built by the Merinides.

Inhabited by 235,000 people, Fez is really three cities: Fez el Bali ("Old Fez"), Fez Djedid ("New Fez," built about 600 years ago), and Ville Nouvelle (a modern residential area). Visitors often tour Fez in a *calèche*, an old horse-drawn vehicle that carries passengers quietly and slowly through the city streets.

THE ATLAS MOUNTAINS

Fez is the door to the Middle Atlas. The road south from the city leads into mountainous country, where the slopes are covered with forests of pine, cedar, and oak. Openings in the trees expose verdant

Above: Fez is the oldest of Morocco's imperial cities. Its yellow mud ramparts enclose a maze of rooftops, towers, and streets. Opposite: In the High Atlas, only the hardiest people live in nearly total isolation. These Berbers are traveling through the mountain pass of Tizi N'Tichka, high in the Atlas Mountains.

meadows where cows and sheep graze the long grass while shepherds doze nearby. The many streams and springs teem with trout. A stream pours over rocks in the thick forest only to fall off a sheer cliff, touching ground hundreds of feet below. There are flashes of color as birds fly into the branches: doves, partridges, woodpeckers, and swallows. A monkey's blatant scream, as the animal swings among the branches, breaks the stillness of the forest. A small caravan of djellaba-clad Berbers on their way to market walks beside overladen donkeys.

This is the heart of Berber country. High in the mountains, the Berbers are isolated from the rest of the world—and they like it that way. These stalwart mountain people value their freedom highly. When neighboring peoples attacked in the past, these Berbers drove them away. They even resisted conquest by the powerful French armies. Determined to defend their land, they built fortresses of red mud, stationing men on the rooftops and on the high walls.

The southern slopes of the Middle Atlas rise into the fiercely savage and wild High Atlas, where only the hardiest people live in nearly total isolation. In winter, snow falls rapidly here in great flakes, quickly burying both man and animal. Some of the highest peaks are covered with snow all year.

Descending from the High Atlas, gorges cut into the land. Narrow canyons wind and twist; their walls are sheer cliffs that rise a thousand feet, revealing only a piece

of the sky. The gorges lead to Tinerhir, a village in the foothills of the Atlas halfway between the Atlantic coast and the Algerian border. In the valley, rivers nurture palm trees, emerald-green grass, and fields of golden wheat.

THE SAHARA

Beyond the foothills the land changes abruptly. This is the beginning of the *hammadas*, or rocky plateaus—land that makes up four fifths of the entire Sahara. The hammadas is a rough, wild region lacking water, and here vegetation ends. Beyond the oasis village of Erfoud lies the vast Sahara. The blazing sun dries up anything that might attempt to live in this bleak land of shifting, white sand dunes and stony hammadas. Only the occasional oases, filled with date palms, break up the sea of white. This is the land of nomads who travel throughout the desert, stopping at the oases for shade, water, and salt. Directly east from Erfoud, across 250 miles of desert, is the oasis of Figuig, the easternmost point of Morocco.

DRAÂ VALLEY

A long, narrow oasis follows the Draâ River system from the Atlas Mountains west through the desert to the Atlantic Ocean. The Draâ Valley is covered with date palms and desert shrubs. More than three hundred varieties of dates are found here. Orange, lemon, almond, and olive trees are cultivated in the valley, and wheat and barley grow along the river banks. Fortified villages, or *ksours*, are built on high ground near the valleys. Inside the high red walls, only slits open out of the massive towers, letting in air but keeping out heat. North of the valley, white sand blows into dunes, their shapes changing every day; to the south lie the unmoving hammadas.

About fifty miles north of where the Draâ River reaches the Atlantic in southern Morocco is the oasis village of Goulimine. This is the home of the "Blue Men," a nomad group whose skins have become pigmented over the centuries with the blue dye they use on their clothing. Further north, past the desert, scrubby vegetation appears on the hills of the Anti-Atlas that can be seen in the distance.

ATLANTIC OCEAN

The road north passes through the town of Agadir, which was built around a bay. The clear blue water of the bay offers excellent swimming. Continuing north, the road becomes progressively hillier to the town of Essaouira, where the Atlas Mountains meet the ocean. The site of an old fishing harbor, Essaouira is built on a rocky peninsula. White houses with blue shutters stand out against the deep blue sea. This city has an interesting history: Hanno, the Carthaginian explorer-writer,

Berber horsemen enter a ksour in southern Morocco.

settled here in the fifth century B.C. while exploring the Atlantic coast. Later, Roman settlers discovered they could extract purple dye from certain mollusks found in the ocean. So they set up a dye factory, dyeing Roman robes purple and sending them back to Rome.

The Anti-Atlas mountains meet the ocean at Essaouira. In the Anti-Atlas are valleys of pink oleanders (poisonous evergreen shrubs), almond trees, roses, the rare carob with its long, black pods, and the argan tree, unique to this area. Goats sit in the branches of the argan, eating the juicy leaves and the yellow fruit. Local Berbers gather the fruit pits from the goat dung and press them to extract the oil, which they use in cooking and on salads.

The next town north is the port of Safi, which ships more sardines than any other port in the world. Early each morning, crowds of people gather at the fish market, shouting their bids as the sardines caught the night before are auctioned off.

Miles of sandy beaches stretch along this part of the Atlantic coast. No one swims here, though, because of the heavy undertow. But a hundred miles north of Essaouira, at El-Jadida, there is fine swimming again. North of the city, trails lead through the rich pine forests to long stretches of uninhabited beach.

CASABLANCA

Casablanca is Morocco's industrial and commercial center. It is by far the largest port in the country—70 percent of Morocco's shipping is handled here. More phosphates are shipped from Casablanca than from any other port in the world. Forty ships can be docked here at one time. While locomotives, farm machinery, and tourists are being unloaded from foreign ships, oranges, olive oil, cork, and sardines are being loaded. On conveyors, quarter-mile-long bins of white phosphate dust are stuffed into foreign freighters.

The earliest settlement in the country was at Casablanca, first called Anfa. The Portuguese destroyed the city in 1468, reoccupying the area a century later and calling it Casa Branco ("White House"). The city was abandoned in 1755 when a big earthquake struck. Two years later, Moors settled there, calling it Dar el Beida. At the end of the eighteenth century, the Spanish came there to trade and gave it the name Casa Blanca.

Today Casablanca is the largest city in Morocco, with a population of more than one million. Traffic jams, factories, and skyscrapers give the city a European character. Near the harbor is an eighteenth-century mosque and surrounding *medina*. A medina can be found in almost every good-sized Moroccan city. It surrounds the main mosque of the town and might have one or more additional mosques within its boundaries. The medina was where the faithful first lived when the town was founded.

A few miles north of Casablanca is Mohammedia, a favorite tourist spot because of its good beaches. It is also one of Morocco's major ports.

THE RED CITY

About 150 miles south of Casablanca, past miles of rich farmland, is Marrakech, a city of 255,000 people. Because the city has long red ramparts, built by the Almoravides, it is often called "The Red City." Marrakech has many gardens and miles of palm groves. Many roads fan out from Marrakech to the interior of the country. Over the Atlas Mountains that rise south of the city, mountain Berbers and Saharan nomads travel to meet and sell their goods in this large metropolis.

Marrakech has a great medina that is a labyrinth of winding streets. In the medina are old, luxurious palaces and mosques as well as the Saadian tombs. In the center of Marrakech is the Djemaa el-Fna Square, whose name means "Assembly of the Dead." The name is appropriate, for once in the city's history, a cruel sultan displayed each week the heads of executed

Opposite top: The port of Casablanca is the largest port in Morocco.
Opposite bottom: Casablanca is Morocco's industrial and commercial center.

Marrakech, "The Red City," lies at the foot of the Atlas Mountains.

rebels—as a warning to others who might dare to oppose him.

Today the square is colorful and joyous. It comes alive every morning when shopkeepers open their windows, the smell of cooking permeates the air, and when merchants set up their tents, arranging their goods on carpets. Artisans work in one section, and porters jog back and forth, bringing them new materials and taking finished works away to be sold. At noon, the crowds retreat from the hot sun into houses, where they eat and sleep. Later in the afternoon, after the heat of the day, the city reawakens. Performers come to the square to entertain; there are musicians, dancers, storytellers, acrobats, snake charmers, sword swallowers, and trained monkeys. With the onset of evening, everyone leaves the marketplace, tents are taken down, and shops are closed.

The marketplace is the "soul of Morocco." Every city has a large *souk* (the Arabic word for "market") open every day, which attracts both city and village people. In rural areas, souks are held in fields on a certain day each week. Merchants travel from souk to souk, selling their goods. Farmers bring produce and shepherds bring livestock. Souks are noisy, bustling places filled with laughter, gossip, shouting, and bargaining. They are the life and enchantment of Morocco.

Handy Reference Section

INSTANT FACTS

Political:
Official Name—The Kingdom of Morocco
Capital—Rabat
Form of Government—Constitutional monarchy
Monetary Unit—*Dirham* (one dirham=100 Moroccan francs=U.S. $.20)
Official Language—Arabic
Official Religion—Islam
Flag—Red with green five-pointed star in center

Geographical:
Area—172,414 square miles
Highest Point—Djebel Toubkal (13,600 feet)
Lowest Point—Sea level
Greatest Width (east to west)—about 760 miles
Greatest Length (north to south)—about 437 miles

POPULATION

Total Population—16,561,000 (1974 estimate)
Population Density—96 persons per square mile

Population of Principal Cities:

Casablanca	1,085,000
Rabat	266,000
Marrakech	255,000
Fez	235,000
Meknès	185,000
Tangier	110,000

ARAB AND BERBER VOCABULARY

Allah=God
Arba=four; Wednesday
babouches=slippers
dahir=royal law
dar=castle
diffa=meal
djebel=mountain
djellaba=hooded cloak
gabbadh=camel cowboy
guedra=family cooking pot
hammadas=pre-Saharan land
Had=one; Sunday
imam=religious leader
inch Allah=if God wills
Inine=two; Monday
Jemaa=six; Friday
khemis=five; Thursday
ksours=fortified villages
la bes=hello
marabout=holy man; local saint
medina=medieval part of city
mezian=very good
oued=river
salaam=peace (used as greeting)
sebt=seven; Saturday
shoukran=thank you
sidi=master
sirocco=Saharan wind
souk=marketplace
Tleta=three; Tuesday

NATIONAL DAYS

March 3—*Fête du Trône*
April 12—*Aid al-Kabir* (Abraham's sacrifice)
June—Feast of Cherries (held at Sefrou)
July 9—Hassan III's birthday
August 20—Revolt of the king and the people (exile of Muhammad V)
October—Feast of Dates (held at Erfoud)
November 18—Independence Day
Many Moroccan holidays vary each year. These holidays are celebrated according to the lunar calendar:

10th day of *Muharram* (1st month)—*Ashura* (beginning of Muslim year)
12th day of *Rebia el Ouel* (3rd month)—*Mulud* (Prophet's birthday)
Ramadan (9th month)—month of fasting
1st day of *Shawwal* (10th month)—*Aid es Seghir* ("The Little Feast Day")
10th day of *Dhul Hi ja* (12th month)—*Aid el Kebir* ("The Feast of Sheep")

YOU HAVE A DATE WITH HISTORY

c. 5000 B.C.—Berbers roam North Africa
146 B.C.—Romans defeat Carthage
45 B.C.—Romans found Africa Nova
40 A.D.—Africa Nova divided into two provinces: western part becomes Mauretania Tingitana
c. 300 A.D.—Berber resistance causes Romans to retreat to Tangier
570—Muhammad, founder of Islam, born
622—Islam founded
683—Arabs first enter Morocco via Taza Gap
c. 700—Arab armies conquer Morocco
mid-700s—Islam splits into two sects
740—Berbers revolt against Omayyad caliph
750—Abassids overthrow Omayyads in Middle East
756—Omayyad empire founded at Cordova, Spain
785—Shiites revolt against Abassids in Middle East, revolt fails; Shiite leader Idris I flees to Morocco, converting many Berbers
c. 800—Fez founded
859—Karaouine University at Fez founded
c. 900—Idrisid dynasty falls
c. 900-1000—Berber rivalry in Morocco
mid-1000s—*Ribat* (retreat) marking start of Almoravid dynasty takes place

1084—Almoravides unify Morocco under Islam
c. 1100—Muhammad ibn-Tubart preaches revolt against Almoravides forming Almohades
1147—Almohades attack Marrakech, conquer Almoravides
1150—Construction of Rabat begun
1269—Beni Merin (Merinides) capture Marrakech
1276—Merinid dynasty assumes power
1465—Beni Wattas assume power
1511—Saadian sherif leads jihad against Portuguese
1549—Saadians capture Fez; Saadian dynasty begins
1578—Moulay Ahmad al-Mansur becomes sultan
mid-1600s—Moulay Rashid captures northern Morocco, becomes first Alaouite sultan
mid-1600s—Moriscos form The Republic of the Two Shores near Rabat and Salé
1670—Alaouites assume power
1672—Moulay Ismail becomes sultan
1757—Sidi Muhammad Ben Abdallah puts down Berber revolts, becomes ruler
1767—Treaty signed with French
1786—Treaty of Marrakech signed with U.S.
1836—Treaty of Meknès signed with U.S.

1873—Moulay Hassan takes throne

1880—Madrid Conference held

1908—Moulay Hafid comes to power, asks for French military assistance; Spain captures Moroccan towns; Germany sends warship into Moroccan bay

1911—German-French agreement: France gets rights to Morocco, November 30

1912—Treaty of Fez signed, setting up French protectorate March 30; General Louis Lyautey appointed resident general; Tangier becomes international zone

1912—Spanish protectorate established November; city of Ifni becomes sovereign Spanish territory

1913—Kenitra founded

1913—Rabat becomes capital

1920—Middle Atlas surrenders to French

1920s—Salafiya religious reform movement begins at Karaouine University; Salafiya opens Arab schools

1924—Abd-el-Krim attacks Fez

1925—Lyautey replaced as resident general; nationalist movement begins at Rabat

1930—Berber dahir leads to demonstrations

1934—Nationalist demonstrations in honor of Sultan Sidi Muhammad ben Yussef; CAM nationalist organization tries to obtain political reforms

1936—CAM splits into two factions: Popular Movement and National Party

1937—Popular Movement and National Party leaders exiled

1938—Private schools in Arabic for Moroccan children begun

1939—World War II begins

1943—Casablanca Conference held; Allies land in Morocco

1944—French schools begin teaching Arabic

1944—Nationalists form Istiglal, January; Istiglal states reforms; Istiglal leaders arrested

1945—World War II ends

1946—Resident general Erik Labonne introduces reforms; Sultan Sidi Muhammad refuses to sign *dahirs* (decrees)

1947—Sidi Muhammad goes to Tangier; riot breaks out in Casablanca; Labonne replaced by Alphonse Juin

1950—Sidi Muhammad goes to Paris to discuss government crisis

1950—Pasha Thami al-Glaoui thrown out of palace for denouncing sultan; attacks Rabat and Fez, forcing sultan to sign dahirs; Istiglal leaders arrested; Moroccan National Front formed

1952—al-Glaoui surrounds palace, sultan exiled; Muhammad Moulay Ben Arafa becomes sultan

1955—Army of Liberation formed; Berber tribesmen attack Oued-Zem, killing all French residents, August 20

1956—French-Moroccan Agreement signed March 2

1956—Spanish-Moroccan Agreement signed April 7

1956—Tangier restored to Morocco, October

1956—Army of Liberation becomes part of Royal Moroccan Army

1957—Sultan Sidi Muhammad ben Yussef becomes King Muhammad V

1958—Mouvement Populaire (MP) formed

1959—National Union of Popular Forces (UNFP) formed, January

1960—Muhammad V assumes direct leadership of government as premier, May

1960—King appoints council to draft constitution, November

1961—Muhammad V dies; Moulay Hassan becomes premier and king, March

1961—Operation Schools begins

1961—Radio education program set up

1962—Successful constitutional referendum by King Hassan, December

1962—Television introduced in Morocco

1963—Front for the Defense of Constitutional Institutions (FDIC) formed

1964—Socialist Democratic Party (PSD) formed

1965—Casablanca student demonstrations turn into riots; king declares state of emergency, June 8

1970—New constitution successfully submitted to referendum, July; Istiglal and UNFP form National Front, boycotting elections; state of emergency ends

1971—Unsuccessful *coup d'etat* against King Hassan, July 10

1972—Rebels attempt assassination of king, August 16

Index

Italicized page numbers indicate illustrations.

About the Author: With the publication of his first book for school use when he was twenty, **Allan Carpenter** began a career as an author that has spanned 134 books—eighty-eight of these now in print for Childrens Press alone, with more still to be published in the Enchantment of Africa series. It has been claimed that he has the longest listing of any author of non-fiction in *Books in Print.* After teaching in the public schools of Des Moines, Mr. Carpenter began his long career as an educational publisher at the age of twenty-one when he founded the magazine *Teachers Digest,* which he edited and published for eight years. In the field of educational periodicals, he was responsible for many innovations, some of which helped to revolutionize that branch of publishing. During his many years in publishing, he has perfected a highly organized approach to handling large volumes of factual material: after extensive traveling and having collected all possible materials, he systematically reviews and organizes everything. Whenever he shares the writing tasks with others, he engages in extensive instruction and continuing consultations with his co-authors. From his apartment high in the magnificent John Hancock Building, Allan recalls: "My collection and assimilation of materials on the states and countries began before the publication of my first book." Allan is the founder and president of Carpenter Publishing House and the founder and chairman of the board of Infordata International, Inc., publishers of *Issues in Education* and *Index to U.S. Government Periodicals.* When not writing or traveling, his principal avocation is music. He has been principal bassist of many symphonies, playing under several noted conductors, and he managed the country's leading non-professional symphony for twenty-five years.